THE DAM BUSTER RAID

THE DAM BUSTER RAID

RAID

A Reappraisal, 70 Years On

Alan W. Cooper

Pen & Sword
AVIATION

First Published in Great Britain in 2013 by
Pen & Sword Aviation
an imprint of
Pen & Sword Books Ltd
47 Church Street, Barnsley, South Yorkshire S70 2AS

ISBN 978-1-78159-474-2

A CIP catalogue record for this book is
available from the British Library.

Typeset in 11/13pt Palatino by
Concept, Huddersfield

Printed and bound in England by
CPI Group (UK) Ltd, Croydon, CR0 4YY

Pen & Sword Books Ltd incorporates the imprints of Pen & Sword
Archaeology, Atlas, Aviation, Battleground, Discovery, Family History,
History, Maritime, Military, Naval, Politics, Railways, Select, Social History,
Transport, True Crime, and Claymore Press, Frontline Books, Leo Cooper,
Praetorian Press, Remember When, Seaforth Publishing and Wharncliffe.

For a complete list of Pen & Sword titles please contact
PEN & SWORD BOOKS LIMITED
47 Church Street, Barnsley, South Yorkshire, S70 2AS, England
E-mail: enquiries@pen-and-sword.co.uk
Website: www.pen-and-sword.co.uk

Contents

Dedication

This book is not to decide if the dams raid was a great success or not, but to make sure all 133 men, and particular the fifty-three who died, are always remembered for their bravery and the great sacrifice they made to make sure that we stayed free; and not under the threat of a regime that had not been seen previously, or we hope never is seen again.

Acknowledgements

My grateful thanks to: David Worrow; Paul Morley; Dave Birrell; Mike Evans; Yasmin Ellis; Mrs Trixie Heveron; Charles Foster; Hartley Garshowitz; Dominic Howard; Darryl Nugent; Dr Albert Speer.

Ken Patterson for his great help in making sure with an expert eye that the book was kept on the straight and level.

Publications:
Dambuster Crash Sites – Chris Ward & Andreas Wachtel
The Men Who Breached The Dams – Alan Cooper.

And my wife Hilda for continued support and help whenever it was asked for.

Introduction

Seventy years ago, in May 1943, an operation was carried out by the RAF which has now become one of the most memorable actions of the Second World War. It was carried out as just another way of contributing to the end of the war in Europe.

The raid on the Ruhr dams in Germany was this operation. It was the beginning of Bomber Command becoming a force to be reckoned with.

Why? It was carried out at a crucial point in the air war, during the air battle of the Ruhr. It showed that targets in the heart of Germany would be hit and were not impregnable. It was an Airborne Commando raid carried out by 133 men, was it a success?

With the heavy casualties involved, there are some who would say No! Three dams were attacked, two were breached. But it has to be pointed out that Barnes Wallis said his bouncing bomb was not suitable for use on the third dam – the Sorpe – because of its construction, earth not masonry. He also said that once you create a weapon and hand it over to the military you do lose control, to some aspect, on its use. We should also put on record that he was not behind the attack on the Sorpe dam.

However, looking at the other side of the coin, the RAF, because of the element of surprise, would only get one shot at breaching the dams; this element of surprise was a big factor

CHAPTER 1

The Dams

What was the reason for the attack on the Ruhr Dams in May 1943?

In October 1937, a list of plans known as the Western Air (WA) Plans was compiled by the Air Staff, for use in the event of war. One of these plans was WA5; attacks on German War Industry, including oil supply, in particular to the Ruhr, Rhineland and Saar.

From an in-depth study of dams, reservoirs and aqueducts as potential pre-war targets the Ruhr dams were identified as possible targets.

The idea to attack the German dams in the Ruhr was discussed by the Air Ministry's Bombing Committee in March 1938. This committee was formed in the 1930s with the idea of studying and accessing how Great Britain could hit, damage or destroy, vital German targets and weaken Germany's ability to wage war. There were many targets listed, discussed and agreed upon. Many could be attacked with conventional bombing; others, which were of a more complicated nature, would need specialized treatment.

On 15 July 1938 the economic and strategic importance of dams was discussed by the Plans Operations at the Air Ministry.

Attacking the dams situated in South Westphalia was discussed in committee on 26 July 1938, the objectives were clear:

(a) Cut off essential supplies of water for industrial and domestic purposes.

(b) Cause flooding and damage to industrial plants, railways, waterways, etc. in the river valley.

(c) And/or to prevent the maintenance of sufficient water for navigation in the inland waterways system.
To make one ton of steel required 150 tons of water.

1

The Ruhr dams were:

> The Mohne – situated in the Mohne Valley south-east of Dortmund, whose role was to collect rainfall to prevent winter flooding and to provide power for electrical generators. Of utmost importance was the part it played in sustaining the underground water supply vital for industrial and household supplies.

> The Eder – situated south of Kassel and south-east of the Mohne. It was built to act as a reservoir for the important Mittelland Canal that runs from the Ruhr to Berlin. It also prevented flooding of farmland in winter and finally served hydroelectrical power stations.

> The Sorpe, Ennepe and Lister dams – situated south of Dortmund and south-west of the Mohne. The roles of these dams were similar to that of the Mohne.

In total there were seven dams in South Westphalia, but the Mohne, Eder, Sorpe and Ennepe were considered of prime importance. The

The Ennepe Dam today. © *After the Battle Magazine*

destruction of the outstandingly important Mohne Dam, with its massive loss of hydroelectric power, would have serious repercussions on the production output from the Ruhr, Germany's major industrial area.

It was decided that the best time for an attack on the dams would be after a period of heavy rain when the reservoirs were full; to breach the dams when low with water would be more difficult than if they were full. If the Mohne dam was breached, the 130 million cubic metres of water contained in this dam would flow down the Ruhr Valley in hours and be so powerful that all villages and towns, as well as waterways in its wake, would be swept away and destroyed. The loss of water from the dam would mean four to five million people would be without water, and the mines and coke plants would come to a standstill owing to the lack of an industrial water supply.

The main problem was how to attack the dams. Normal conventional bombing would only chip the top of the dams; attack by torpedo would probably be thwarted by torpedo nets.

This meant that an attack on the Ruhr dams was mothballed for a time until some form of weapon, or attack, was designed. An idea of a method of attack did come to light not long after the Second World War began. But as with many things, it was not really taken seriously. At the time, the Controller of Armament Research and Development at the British firm of Messrs Vickers Armstrong Ltd, Weybridge, was Dr Barnes Wallis. He, with his scientific brain, had come up with an idea. He was 52 when the war began in September 1939 and had a background of success, he designed the successful Airship R100 which flew to Canada and back, but when the Government R101 airship crashed, all airships and development was stopped and the R100 broken up. He also developed the geodetic method of construction used in the Wellesley and Wellington bombers. Many a crew owed much to this method of construction in getting back to the UK after being damaged. The idea was that when an aircraft was hit, much of the flak or fighter firepower would go through the intertwined basket-like fuselage, and not damage any vital parts of the bomber.

Wallis was already aware of the importance of the Ruhr dams. In 1939, German bombers were dropping 500lb bombs on London and causing great damage, particularly since they usually exploded deep inside a building. In this Wallis found the answer to the problem; it lay in an anti-submarine depth charge which was detonated

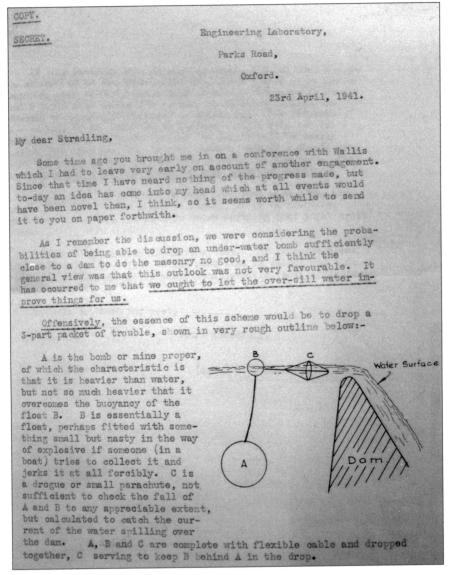

COPY.

SECRET.

Engineering Laboratory,

Parks Road,

Oxford.

23rd April, 1941.

My dear Stradling,

Some time ago you brought me in on a conference with Wallis which I had to leave very early on account of another engagement. Since that time I have heard nothing of the progress made, but to-day an idea has come into my head which at all events would have been novel then, I think, so it seems worth while to send it to you on paper forthwith.

As I remember the discussion, we were considering the probabilities of being able to drop an under-water bomb sufficiently close to a dam to do the masonry no good, and I think the general view was that this outlook was not very favourable. It has occurred to me that we ought to let the over-sill water improve things for us.

Offensively, the essence of this scheme would be to drop a 3-part packet of trouble, shown in very rough outline below:-

A is the bomb or mine proper, of which the characteristic is that it is heavier than water, but not so much heavier that it overcomes the buoyancy of the float B. B is essentially a float, perhaps fitted with something small but nasty in the way of explosive if someone (in a boat) tries to collect it and jerks it at all forcibly. C is a drogue or small parachute, not sufficient to check the fall of A and B to any appreciable extent, but calculated to catch the current of the water spilling over the dam. A, B and C are complete with flexible cable and dropped together, C serving to keep B behind A in the drop.

Wallis' idea to breach the dams. © *National Archives*

under water. This destroyed by means of shock waves transmitted by the water itself and not by the blast.

On 2 April 1940, the Wing Commander Assistant Superintendent of the Research Department wrote to the Commander-in-Chief of Bomber

Command, Air Marshal Sir Richard Peirse, saying that on his visit to Bomber Command he was sorry he had missed seeing him. The subject of his visit was attacks on dams in enemy territories. The principle one, he said, was the Mohne in the Ruhr. As he thought it would be heavily defended, the attack would have to be from a distinct height. Its destruction would flood the Ruhr Valley and disorganize its industries. He went on to say that no weapon existed to attack the face of the dam, but he said that a weapon was being considered, thanks to the development of this department and the Navy.

Group Captain Frederick Winterbotham, who was a member of the Air Staff at the Air Ministry, acknowledged that there was something in Wallis' thinking, and he would try to convince the Air Staff that a penetrating bomb may well be the answer to breaching the dams. He did this by going to the top, Desmond Morton, who was on the Prime Ministers staff. If Morton became interested he would go to Professor Linderman (Later Baron Cherwell), who was also a personal assistant, to the Prime Minister.

A reply came on 5 July 1940. Linderman's reply was to Wallis disappointing, as it stated that his idea would not come to fruition until 1942, if then. However, Wallis, supported by Winterbotham, kept researching the project. This persistence paid off as he persuaded the Ministry of Aircraft Production that the chance of destroying a large dam in Germany was worth looking into.

In October 1940, Barnes Wallis put to Dr David Pye, the Director of the Department of Scientific Research, his theory on the destruction of enemy dams and the need to experiment with models. This was accepted and agreed, the experiments were to be made with the Road Research Laboratory branch of the Scientific and Industrial Research and the Ministry of Home Security, under the supervision of Dr W.R. Glanville, head of the branch. Early tests using gelignite in the vicinity of concrete pipes, moulded as arches, seem to bear out Mr Wallis's calculations regarding multiple arch dams.

In November 1940, Mr Wallis was given access to a report prepared for the Air Ministry in 1939 on the construction of the Mohne Dam. It had been prepared by Sir William Halcrow, a member of the Institute of Civil Engineers.

This contained no detail of the dam's construction, but research by Wallis into German technical papers prepared at the time of its being built, obtained from the library of the Institute of Civil Engineers, gave him the information he needed for the construction of a series of models. These, and others prepared by the Road Research Laboratory after similar research, played an important part in the experiments which were about to begin.

The attack, if successful, had to be made at the water face side of the dam; a charge, which had still to be determined, would be placed at a maximum distance below the water level, and at some distance from the base of the dam.

In a letter of 20 December 1940, the Birmingham Water Department agreed to allow the Ministry of Home Security to have – for experimental purposes – the disused dam at Nant-Y-Gro, in Wales. The Water Department understood that the dam would be destroyed, but they would not require its reinstatement. It also offered all facilities to the site, and for further arrangements to be made direct with Mr Barnes.

Both the Mohne and Eder Dams were gravity types, so it was thought tests on a scale model of the dams had question marks against them. But tests were arranged under the guidance of Dr William Glanville,

Tests at Nant-Y-Gro Dam. © *National Archives*

Tests at Nant-Y-Gro Dam. © *National Archives*

who had much experience in the results of explosives. With a model basic rules were simple, the model would be of the same material as the dam and the results would be the same if the weight of the explosives were produced by the cube of the scale ratio. One must bear in mind that the idea of a bouncing bomb was not even on the horizon at this stage.

The Mohne was made of rubble masonry laid in cement mortar and more solid than the Eder, it had a sealing bank of clay at its base on the upstream face, so was chosen as the prototype for production, on a ratio of 1:50. The models were built by Dr's Davey and A.J. Newman; their efforts can still be seen today at the Building Research Establishment.

The first test was made with a 56g charge at a distance of 9 metres – about 29 feet, which was equivalent, on the full scale, of 45 metres from the upstream face – about 165 feet. This resulted in cracks in the dam wall, with a vertical crack at the centre and a horizontal one under the crest.

For both the Mohne and Eder Dams, the charge required to produce an effective breach was estimated to be in the region of 3,600kg, and

A series of shots of the tests carried out at Nant-Y-Gro Dam. © *National Archives*

Tests at Nant-Y-Gro dam. © *National Archives*

should explode 9 metres below the water. It was essential the aircraft would be able to obtain a direct hit. The problem still was how to obtain this direct hit, at this time there was no means of obtaining this with current aiming methods. Despite this, Barnes Wallis kept working at evolving a secret plan he had.

He contacted Group Captain Winterbotham with the idea of a spherical bomb, detonated so that the explosion would reach all points of the surface at the same moment. Winterbotham asked Wallis if a round bomb would penetrate deep enough to do any real damage with a shock wave. He was keen to know if there was any data at the Air Ministry on this subject, so Winterbotham rang the Air Ministry to ask what the effect of dropping a large spherical bomb from about ten thousand feet would be. The reply was, it would bounce along like a football but without any accuracy. Surprisingly, Wallis thought this to be 'Splendid.'

He then asked Winterbotham for a set of drawings for the new Avro Lancaster bomber. This was about to come into service very shortly. It was a four engine bomber version of the two engine Manchester, which had proved a failure, due mainly to lack of power.

Wallis also told him he had spent a whole day on the terrace of his home, shooting glass marbles over the surface of the water in a tin bath, his children, Mary and Christopher, helped with great gusto. It was always a contentious subject post-war between these two as to whose marbles they were.

There was by now interest in the Ministry of Aircraft Production, to form an 'Air Attack on the Dams Committee', they played a helpful role in what happened later, and not as the film seemed to portray, that they were counter-productive.

On 24 December 1940, there was a meeting of experts and Mr Barnes Wallis. The conclusion of this meeting regarding gravity dams was that it was necessary to check the validity of small model tests by carrying out a large scale test, if a suitable dam could be found. It was decided to carry out laboratory tests on models which could be later utilized for large scale tests, one of the members present, Dr Stradling, mentioned the disused dam at Nant-Y-Gro, in Wales.

This was of great interest to the Ministry of Home Security, who were concerned about their own water storage and supplies, but within a few days permission had been obtained from the Birmingham City Corporation to use the dam for destruction tests, and the site was inspected by several experts who had been at the meeting. Drawings and details of constructions were provided and the Road Research Laboratory arranged for models to be made. Dr Stradling wrote on 3 January 1941 to Sir Henry Tizard, Scientific Advisor to the Chief of the Air Staff at the Ministry of Aircraft Production (M.A.P.), outlining the latest proposals and asked for the backing of the Ministry. This was duly given and with the Ministry now officially interested in developing plans, they went ahead with the Nant-Y-Gro dam experiments.

In February 1941 further tests were made against a 1/50th scale model of the Mohne Dam: arrangements for these having been made some months previously. These tests confirmed the earlier deduction; that a large quantity of explosives would be necessary if serious damage was to be caused. The model would have every known detail of the dam, this entailed making hundreds of blocks measuring $0.4 \times 0.3 \times 0.2$ inches and laying them in courses of fine cement mortar with a thin coat of rendering over the whole.

The building of this accurate model, replacing all the models used in the long series of experiments, was the work of the building research station at Watford, and designs which resulted from the collaboration of the Road Research Laboratory and Mr Wallis.

On 10 March 1941 came the first meeting of the Air Attack on Dams Committee, they discussed the experiments to date in great detail; in particular, what further model experiments were necessary and to make arrangements for full scale experiments. The committee was chaired by David Pye, with Dr Glanville, Dr Reginald Stradling (later Sir), Mr Horace Morgan, Professor Desmond Bernal, Professor W.R. Thomas and Barnes Wallis.

A paper had been written 'A note on a method of attacking the Axis Powers', which included details of a ten-ton bomb, and a sketch of the bomb, for a possible attack on the Mohne Dam, later known as Upkeep.

At the end of 1941, Dr Reginald Stradling, who was a member of this committee, and with the consent of the Birmingham Corporation, suggested to the committee that the small Nant-Y-Gro dam in the Elan Valley, which had been built at the end of the eighteenth century and provided water for the construction of the Elan Valley dams, but was now no longer required, might be suited to test the gravitational effects of scale. It was about 10 metres high (35 feet) and 16 metres (55 feet) wide, of the straight gravity design and made of mass concrete. It was in a remote locality, and could be breached safely, with the water to run harmlessly into the Caban-Coch reservoir.

However, because of its remoteness the bomb had to be man-handled to the location. This was done with the help of the Royal Engineers using a small boat; the bomb was suspended three metres below the water level. Two high-speed cinematograph cameras and their operators were provided by the Royal Aircraft Establishment, and arrangements were made to record pressures and movements.

In January 1942 it was agreed that the dams were a profitable target. Wallis passed his idea on to a friend, Professor P.S. Blackett, who passed it on to Sir Henry Tizard, who arranged for the use of two large experimental ship-testing tanks at the National Physical Laboratory at Teddington and gave the new scheme his full support, as did the Department of Scientific Research. No. 1 tank was 550 feet in length and the smaller of the two; it was used if the larger one was not available. No. 2 tank was 640 feet long, 23 feet wide and 9 feet deep.

Wallis built a model dam which was submerged in the tank and catapulted two-inch wooden-balls at it, with a girl cinematographer submerged in an airtight glass tank filming the spinning spheres as the balls hit the tank. The balls were of different weights and sizes. From this he had to accurately calculate ratios of weight, size and speed to the length of bounce before any further progress could be achieved. Sir Henry Tizard came to watch these trials and after two days a pattern of bounce began to emerge. Wallis had finally managed to put a backspin on the ball and to come near enough in his calculations to predict, with some accuracy, the outcome of a bouncing bomb attack from the air on a dam wall. The tests went well and gave great hope for further tests.

On 26 February 1942, Wallis, Verity, and Craven went to see Air Marshal Linnell. Wallis had met him in the early stages of his experiments. He told them all that testing and development of the bomb with the use of the Avro Lancaster was to proceed at once. The Air Staff have ordered, he said, 'that you are to be given everything you want.' He promised three Lancaster's modified by Avro's.

Wallis was going back and forth between his drawing office at Surhill, Woolwich – it was here that the bombs were filled – and the experimental dropping ground at Reculver Bay, near Margate in Kent. After all his efforts it seemed at last it would come to fruition.

In April 1942, Mr Wallis produced a paper describing his special weapon. This dealt mainly with the carriage of the mine in the aircraft, air ballistics and underwater path, and showed that while the bomb was unsuitable for penetration bombing, it was suitable for underwater action.

The first live explosive was made at the Elan Valley on 22 May 1942 and watched by Barnes Wallis. This proved to be spectacular, but not seriously damaging the dam. After further work on the bomb, or mine, another attempt was made in July of the same year when a mine was suspended at the optimum depth (by scaffolding) from the mid-point of the 180 feet long dam and detonated.

On 21 June 1942, following a demonstration at Teddington and witnessed by several officials of the M.A.P, the Controller of Research and Development wrote to D.S.R saying, 'I consider that the model experiments have established a clear case for an air test using full-scale missiles. I therefore authorize the institution of such trials and agree to allocation of a Wellington aircraft fitted for the carriage of 4,000lb H.C. bombs. I understand the structural modifications to the aircraft are relatively small, in that they are concerned only with the modification of the bomb bay fairing.'

The area for the trials had been decided upon on 25 August 1942. The area chosen was a strip of water twelve miles long off Chesil Beach, West of Portland. The date set for the end of September 1942. This would be delayed until the tests in Wales had been completed.

By the middle of September 1942, the first experimental empty mines had been made at Messrs Vickers's Armstrong Works and eleven were under construction.

In Wales, another attempt was made in July 1942, when a mine was suspended at the correct depth (by scaffolding) from the mid-point of the 180 feet long dam and detonated remotely. The result; a huge central section of the dam wall was successfully blasted in a massive explosion. This successful trial confirmed that it was necessary to deliver an explosive device under water and in direct contact with the dam wall in order to breach it.

Wellington Bomber. © *N. Didwell*

Also in July 1942, at a third meeting of the Dams committee, the general opinion was that a dam of that size could not be expected to be completely destroyed by a charge of less than 30,000lbs of explosives placed upstream of the dams and not less than 50 feet from it.

It was obvious that such a charge of that weight could not be carried in any known or contemplated aircraft. Neither could it be dropped with such accuracy at night and in the face of enemy fighters and ground anti-aircraft fire.

The conclusion was that an attack on the Mohne Dam was impracticable with existing weapons, unless multiple charge techniques could be developed. This would prove a long and difficult business and so it was decided that an attack on a gravity dam was a hopeless proposition.

With the knowledge available at the time, their conclusion was that the project could not be justified, but Mr Wallis felt this was not the end of the subject. Certainly not on a subject of such importance.

It now came for the real thing to be tested. But he still had to have Government backing. Once again Winterbotham came to the rescue. He knew the Parliamentary Private Secretary to the Minister of Production, Garro-Jones, also a former R.F.C. pilot. A new committee had recently been set up under the Ministry to examine new and promising projects of this kind. He was so impressed by Wallis's invention that he obtained a hearing with the committee headed by Sir Thomas Merton, the Scientific Advisor to the Ministry of Aircraft Production. The result was the go-ahead to construct and test a prototype bouncing bomb.

Prototype bombs were built and tests made using a Wellington bomber. The first trial took place on 4 December 1942 over Chesil Beach, near Weymouth, Dorset. The pilot was Mutt Summers, Chief Test Pilot for Vickers, with Wallis the bomb aimer on this flight. They flew over the water at very low-level, and at the right moment Wallis pressed the release button. The bomb hit the water but its case crushed slightly on impact – it would have to be made stronger. On 12 December 1942 they tried again and this time it worked. Over the next few days three more bombs were dropped with the tests being recorded by a movie camera.

On 28 January 1943, the Managing Director of Vickers Armstrong, Sir Charles Craven, told Wallis that he was to go to London, as the First Sea Lord, Sir Dudley Pound, wanted to see the films of the Chesil Beach drops. He sat with the Admiral and the film, given the title 'Most Secret Trial Number One' began. It showed a Wellington bomber with a bulge beneath it, the bomb dropped away with a backward spin at considerable speed and fell backwards into the sea. When it hit the water it bounced about a dozen times and covered about a half mile over the surface before it finally sank. Having seen the film the Admiral was very impressed with what he had seen. The Royal Navy were keen to get their hands on such a weapon for use against German battleships such as the *Tirpitz*. But if used, Wallis realized that all element of surprise against the dams would be lost.. He knew that unless he got the Prime Minister on board, and he gave the dam's raid priority, his idea of attacking the Ruhr dams were lost. He contacted Lord Cherwell in an attempt to prevent the navy talking up the bomb for use on German shipping. Wallis sent a twenty page 'secret' report, photographs and diagrams, on the theory of a spinning bomb. Along with a suggestion that the dams be attacked in mid-May 1943, when there was a full moon and not covered by cloud. A meeting with Cherwell on 2 February 1943 followed and again the film was shown, but for some reason nothing came of it.

On 12 February 1943, Wallis wrote a letter to Winterbotham asking for his help. At the same time a campaign was being undertaken to stop the trials on Upkeep. Winterbotham wrote to Air Vice-Marshal Inglis who was able to get to Air Chief Marshal Sir Charles Portal, the Chief of the Air Staff. He seemed in favour of at least looking at the idea.

At a meeting at the Air Ministry on 13 February 1943, a note was made that a spherical bomb – with the code name of Upkeep – was being developed and trialled with mock-up models. This indicated to the committee that the weapon could be successful – if used. The bomb used in the trials was about 36 inches in diameter and it weighed 1,000lbs. Tests were made and carried out with the use of a specially modified Mosquito aircraft. A second meeting was arranged for 15 February, by which time further evidence could be obtained from further tests at the Teddington tanks.

The test was presented at the meeting on the 15 February 1943, it showed the ball finally plunging below the surface and crawling into position against the side of the tank.

On 14 February 1943, an internal letter was sent to the Commander-in-Chief of Bomber Command, Sir Arthur Harris, from his SASO, Air Vice-Marshal Robert Saundby, concerning the meeting on 13 February 1943. The letter outlined the plan to attack the German dams with a bouncing bomb, and concluded that he thought it was possible. He went on to say that one squadron of bombers should have its aircraft modified to carry the weapon and used to attack the dams.

However, this did not convince Harris. He wrote the same day to Saundby.

> 'This is tripe of the wildest description. There are so many "ifs" and that there was not the smallest chance of it work-ing. To begin with, the bomb would have to be perfectly balanced round its axis; otherwise vibration at 500 RPM would wreck the aircraft or tear the bomb loose. I don't believe a word of its supposed ballistics on the surface. It would be much easier to design a bomb to run on the surface, built to nose in on contact, sink and explode. This bomb would of course be heavier than water and exactly fit existing bomb bays.
>
> 'At all costs stop them putting aside Lancasters and reducing our bombing effort on this wild goose chase. Let them prove the practicability of the weapon first. The war will be over before it works – and it never will.'

To be fair to Sir Arthur, it should be remembered that he had many ideas put to him while C-in-C Bomber Command, many of them far-fetched. Everyone seemed to be an expert in bombing Germany. He was concerned that he should not lose any of his precious Lancaster bombers in hair-brained schemes and he was supported in this by the Chief of Air Staff, Sir Charles Portal. Portal had also seen the Chesil Beach films and wrote to Harris assuring him that he would not allow more than three Lancasters to be diverted on tests for the Upkeep bomb.

The Central Intelligence Units (C.I.U.) were based at Medmenham and were designated by single letters of the alphabet: 'D', 'R', 'W', and 'V' and under the command of Wing Commander Kendal. 'D' Section, under Wing Commander Howard Thomas, was responsible for the interpretation of reports; 'R' co-ordinated the demands of those responsible for the planning of operations; 'W' provided the necessary data, such as photographic material and maps at the correct scale for 'V', who produced the scale models of the dams.

On 17 February 1943, a model of the Mohne Dam was delivered to Bomber Command, it had been made by a section known as 'W' at a scale of 1:6,000, and compiled from photographs taken on 4 and 5 September 1941.

On 19 February 1943, the potential justified pressing on with development as soon as possible. The modification of three Lancasters to carry the mines was underway and sufficient modification sets for two squadrons were to be made, and manufacture of 100 mines. Also on 19 February 1943, a special reconnaissance sortie was flown from RAF Benson, this covered the Mohne Dam. A report was made of this sortie by Captain Espenhahn of the Army Section; this covered the defences around the area of the dam and was issued on 21 February 1943.

A second, very detailed report was completed and with it was a plan put together by Flying Officer d'Arcy Smith of 'D' Section, and completed on the 27 February 1943. The result was that the model itself now required certain modifications; these were completed by 3 March 1943. On 4 April 1943, a model of the Sorpe Dam was started, and completed on the 19 April 1943. The model of the Eder Dam was completed on 15 May 1943, only a day before the raid.

On 22 February 1943, Harris was advised that Wallis would visit him with the test film. He arrived along with Mutt Summers and set out to explain his ideas, after which Harris seemed to be more interested and agreed to see the film. The only people present – for security reasons – were Harris, Wallis, Summers and Saundby, who worked the projector, when it finished the only thing Harris promised was to think it over. But then came what seemed to be a U-turn for Wallis, he was summoned to Sir Charles Craven and told to stop all thoughts of attacking the Ruhr Dams. Upon this Wallis resigned, was accused by Craven of mutiny, and left. He then went to see Sir Thomas Morton and told him he had resigned. Sir Thomas's assistant, Sydney Barratt, then spoke to Wallis for over an hour about scientific assistance of his case. The outcome was that Churchill was sent the Upkeep papers. This was a big breakthrough for Wallis, and Churchill, having read through the papers, gave the order for the raid on the German dams to go ahead. This was the very news Wallis had hoped for. After this breakthrough his resignation was not accepted and Wallis was soon back at work on the next stage of the tests. Time was running out and the bomb, or mine, still not perfected, it was now March and the time set for the attack was May. He had been summoned with Verity and Sir Charles Craven to the office of Air Marshal John Linnell OBE, Controller of Research at the Air Ministry, whom Wallis had met during the early days of his experiments. He told them 'the Air Staff have ordered that you be given everything you want' He promised them three modified Lancasters. Plans were made for thirty aircraft to be modified and 150 mines. This was to take precedence over all other requirements, such was the importance of the dam's project. It had now been given the codename Upkeep. Days later Linnell resigned.

As Churchill had given the green light for the operation all obstacles were brushed aside.

Group Captain Verity, in charge of air force intelligence, received a call on his green scrambler telephone. It came from Air Commodore Patrick 'Tubby' Grant, the Deputy Director of Intelligence and his boss informed him that a civilian gentleman named Wallis was visiting him. Not long after the door of Verity's office opened and in bounded Wallis, looking a little dishevelled and with a distinctive shock of white hair. He explained the outline of the operation and the bomb. He showed him all the sketches and left Verity with the impression that he had not only an absorbing man in his office, but a brilliant man.

Verity had been a Chartered Engineer before the war and Wallis thought he would understand how the dams were constructed. He soon got his staff on the case and access to volumes of information dealing with dams and German engineering. They got all the papers etc on the Mohne dams from the library of the Institute of Civil Engineers, so in minutes all details of its design and construction were there to see. For security reasons all his mail went to Effingham Golf Club and no contact was made with him at Vickers or his home. Group Captain Verity then got down to producing some details of the standard target material, maps, information sheets, drawings, photographs, etc.

Barnes Wallis was now working in a drawing office at Surhill, Woolwich – where the bombs were to be filled – and the experimental dropping ground at Reculver Bay, near Margate, Kent. He had persevered to convince all the sceptics that his idea was not only possible, but now coming to fruition.

On 4 March 1943 came a letter from Roy Chadwick who had invented the Lancaster. 'I should like to take the opportunity of saying that this project appears to be of such terrific possibilities that everything humanly possible will be done by us to make our part of the show successful.'

Converting the Lancasters was no mean task. The changes had to be built into the aircraft on the production line.

On 7 March 1943 Wallis was informed that the Upkeep trials were to be held at Reculver Bay. On 12 March 1943, the Research Department decided to form a 'Co-ordination Committee' of various heads of departments in the Ministry of Aircraft Production and Air Staff, among its terms of reference being, 'to co-ordinate the various development and construction programme for which Ministry of Aircraft Production is responsible and to ensure the complete articles arrive at the place and by the date required by the Air Staff.' They would meet once a week, the first aircraft would be ready by 1 April 1943, and the remaining twenty by the end of the month, whilst seventy-five filled mines would also be ready at that time. The Air Staff was asked to select the squadron for the task and from where they would operate.

Three days later the Minister of Aircraft Production wrote, 'there must be no falling down in this programme, which must be regarded as of vital importance.'

On 17 March 1943, it was decided that shifts of twenty-four hours, seven days a week were necessary to complete the work on time.

At the end of March 1943 the position regarding development was that sixty-seven mines were made (forty were being inert filled –

twenty-seven H.E. filled) this implied forty for practice and twenty-seven for use on the operation. The former would have an estimated delivery date of 15 April 1943 and the H.E. (High Explosive) on 8 May 1943. The period 16 April to 12 May 1943 was one of intense activity by the development and trials staff, and the crew of 617 Squadron, a squadron newly formed for this one operation. On 12 May 1943, the Air Staff made a report to the Chiefs of Staff Committee that the weapon and been proved in trials. They immediately sanctioned the operation for an attack on German dams with the special mine. Trial drops of Highball and Upkeep were made on 28 April 1943.

On 6 May 1943 further drops were made in Lancasters ED 765-G and 817-G and again on the 7 May 1943. But it was 13 May 1943 when the drop was the most successful, using a filled and fully armed Upkeep.

On 15 May 1943 a signal was sent by the Assistant Chief of the Air Staff (A.C.A.S) (Ops) to Bomber Command – 'Operation Dambuster, immediate attack on targets "X", "Y", and "Z" approved. Execute at the first suitable opportunity.'

The latest date for the operation to take place was 26 May 1943. The main problem had been time and also keeping the operation a secret. Even the pilots detailed to make reconnaissance flights over the dams, took different routes to avoid creating suspicion. Also, they noticed no difference in the defences, so were sure that the Germans did not suspect anything. But it was a close thing as far as time, in that the last trial was on 13 May 1943.

CHAPTER 2

The Target – Upkeep

The plan, bearing in mind that such an attack would be a one-off, was to attack as many dams as possible, five main German dams. The most important of these five was thought to be the Mohne Dam, a hydroelectric power station at Gunne, six and half miles south-west of Soest, and twenty-five miles east of Dortmund.

The dam was situated at the north-west corner of a reservoir which extends eastwards from the dam for about six miles and south-east for about three and half miles. It had been built to hold a storage capacity of between 13 million and 140 million cubic metres of water and was constructed between 1909 and 1913, in order to improve the flow of the River Ruhr, and by helping with water shortages during summer and autumn. In addition, the numerous pumping stations which provided water for the towns of the Rhine-Westphalia area, as well as hydroelectric plants along the river, could be supplied with adequate water, even during dry periods.

Water was very important to the German armament industry, to produce one ton of steel required 150 tons of water. In comparison, coal mines require one cubic metre of water per ton of coal raised; coke ovens about two cubic metres, while blast furnaces two cubic metres for each ton of iron produced. Additionally, power stations and chemical industries also make heavy demands on water supplies. Taking this on board, the dam was of vital importance to the whole Ruhr Valley; its destruction would cause disastrous flooding and also upset water supplies over a large part of the most mighty industrial area of Germany.

The dam was made of limestone rubble masonry and was specially protected against seepage of water. It was bedded into at least six and half feet of rock at its base and was built in a curve. It was 130 feet high from its rock bottom. Its length was 2,100 feet and its thickness 25 feet at the top and 112 feet at the bottom. The depth of water when full – in the middle of the lake – was 128 feet.

The water was normally drawn off by means of four pipes, 4.62 metres in diameter, carried in pairs through culverts in the foot of the dam. Each pipe had two valves, one serving to discharge the water directly into the Mohne and the other carrying it to the power station. These valves were controlled from the crest of the dam and operated by either electric power or by hand. The control rooms were in the round chambers built on each side of the gable towers on the top of the dam. The power station was directly below the dam, operated by the Vereinigte Elecktrizitaetswerke Westphalia AG (VEW), equipped with two driving turbines, a main turbine of 2,200hp, and an auxiliary turbine of about 1,000hp, at maximum output.

Gravity dams such as the Mohne offer a problem as a target owing to the massive masonry or concrete walls, these are approximately triangular in cross section, resisting the great press of water with its tendency to try and push them downstream. They also cause a problem due to their sheer weight and the fact that they are keyed to the rocky bed of the valley across the outlet from which they stand. The immense strength of the dam was due to its thickness of 112 feet at the base.

The limestone used in the construction was a kind found in the Ruhr Valley, near Neheim Husten, and also a kind of sandstone called greywacke, with a small proportion of green sandstone. The mortar was a cement-trass in proportion of one cement, three white lime, five trass and twelve sand. As opposed to other dams, two rock-sand and not river sand was used, i.e. crushed stone. On the water side, an impregnable coating of half limestone, which would prevent fluid passing through a two and half cement coating, was applied, this was then painted over with two coats of 'Siderostthen' or 'Nigrit'. To protect it against waves, frost, heat from the sun and mechanical damage, the plastered surface had a facing of sixty to ninety centi-metres to the full height. A further wall of clay, two metres thick was rammed halfway up the wall from the valley bottom.

There were twelve dams along the River Ruhr with a full capacity of 200 to 266 million cubic metres. In 1943 the Mohne Dam was estimated to contain 134 million cubic metres, or approximately half of the total of the twelve dams.

The Mohne Dam was protected with two rows of torpedo nets hanging down from floating wooden beams and stretched across the water, 100 to 300 feet out from the top of the dam wall. There was concern in Germany in 1939, by a German Mayor, Duigardt, who expressed concern over the lack of defences for these large Westphalian dams. In a letter to the military authorities in Munster, he pointed out the possible results should the dams be destroyed from the air, not from a direct hit, but by a bomb dropped 20 or 30 metres from the dam, which would explode below the water line! If the charge was large enough the collapse of a dam might be caused owing to compressive effect of the water on the explosive.

If, he went on to say, the Mohne Dam was breached, a volume of water of say a hundred and thirty million cubic metres – depending on the size of the breach – would flood the Ruhr Valley in a few hours. The flood would be that powerful that villages, towns and waterworks in the Ruhr Valley as far as the Rhine would be destroyed by the water. This would paralyse the entire Ruhr area, not only would four to five million people be without water, but mines and coking plants would suddenly cease working owing to the loss of water.

There were some defences with flak guns being installed on the Mohne Dam. In May 1940 these were removed but again reinstated in 1942. There were three 2cm anti-aircraft guns on each tower of the dam and one in the centre of the dam. About 250 metres west of the dam were a further three 2cm anti-aircraft guns. Barrage balloons that had been put there were taken away and not replaced, but there were twenty small balloons distributed in a ring fashion around the dam and 500 metres from it. Some of the balloons were operated from boats. In 1942, a light net was introduced, it was positioned 100 metres east of the dam in the water and was held and strengthened from shore to shore.

The Air Staff expected the destruction of the dam to have serious effects on industrial activity and would greatly affect morale as it was of such huge importance to the water supply of the Ruhr. The Sorpe destruction would further enhance the critical situation in the Ruhr industries and would add greatly to the already affected morale caused by the destruction of the Mohne Dam.

The second target in the Ruhr Valley area, the Sorpe Dam, was built between 1927 and 1935, and made of earth with a concrete core. It had a water volume of 72 million cubic metres and the height of the dam wall was 58 feet. It was situated on the River Sorpe, a tributary of the Ruhr, six miles south of the mighty Mohne Dam and had taken three years to fill. This dam, however, was of a different construction, it was closed by an earth and stone wall with a cement core at the base in which was an inspection gallery. Although chosen as a target, it was not, in the opinion of Barnes Wallis, suitable for his bouncing bomb or mine, being of solid concrete. It was Germany's highest earth dam.

The third dam selected as a target was the Eder. As with the Sorpe, the Eder was situated on the west of the Ruhr. It was situated in the area of the River Eder at Hemforth, about two miles south of Waldeck and twenty-four miles north-west of Bad Wilddungen and built of masonry. Its power station was the 30,000kW Hemforth I and II hydro-electric stations of the Preussische Elektrizitaets AG, and had a water volume of 202 million cubic metres. The Eder Dam was the largest dam in Germany, 139 feet high, 1,310 feet long, with a thickness of 19 feet at the top and 115 feet at the bottom. Its reservoir area was much larger than the Mohne and water capacity was greater in con-sequence – 7,100 million cubic metres. Its purpose was to store water for protection against flooding and for increasing the water flow of the Fulda and Weser Rivers, and the Mittelland Canal, in order to improve navigation.

The attack and destruction of the Eder Dam would result in the destruction of the four associated hydroelectric power stations, one at Hemforth, two at Brenghause, and one at Offolden. Together, they had a total capacity of 150,000 kW, constituting an important item in the electrical supply system of the Preussen Elektra, particularly the Brenghause Station, which was a pump storage peak load plant. The dams' destruction would result in serious flooding and damage to communications and industrial plants on the banks of the river. The Sorpe and Eder were used in conjunction with each other. The Kaiser had visited the dam when it was under construction

On 8 March 1943, the Air Staff forecast that the planned attack on the Eder Dam would have spectacular results and the moral effects would be important if the operation was carried out in conjunction with the two Ruhr dams, the Mohne and Sorpe. But the economic effect however, was unlikely to be substantial.

The fourth dam, the Ennepe, was built between 1902 and 1905 in the Arnsberg area. This dam was sometimes referred to as the Schelme. Its water volume was 15 million cubic metres, and its walls were of masonry, its height was 45 feet. The fifth dam, the Lister, was built between 1909 and 1911 in Attendorn, again built of masonry and to a height of 35 feet. Its capacity was 22 million cubic metres of water.

The weapon, a bomb, or known in the records as a mine, was sixty inches or five feet long and fifty inches in diameter. It had three hydrostatic pistols set to detonate at 30 feet, also a ninety-second time-fuse, initiated at release, indented to destroy the weapon if for any reason the pistols failed to function. One of the bombs, or mine, did not detonate when one of the aircraft crashed, so this was not infallible. On each end of the cylindrical casing was a hollow circular tract, twenty inches in diameter, into which disc-like wheels were mounted on supporting calliper arms and fitted with fore and aft axis. These callipers were designed by Barnes Wallis himself. It had a total weight of 9,250lbs, which consisted of 6,600lbs RDX charge weight and 2,650lbs of bomb casing, mechanism, etc. It looked like the front wheel of a steamroller. The pistols were of a Royal Navy standard Mk XIV and used in depth charges.

A safety pin was attached to a wire which in turn was attached to one of the calliper arms to release the bomb when the bomb aimer pressed his release button in the normal way. When activated, the calliper arms holding each side of the bomb were forced open by powerful springs, and away went the bomb. It was driven by a Vickers–Jassey Variable Speed hydraulic motor with a belt drive, attached to one of the discs. The motor was started seven minutes before arrival at the target and rotation controlled at 500 rpm. This motor was used in submarines in the 1930 to 1945 period. The wireless-operator controlled the speed of the motor; a rev counter from a motorbike was used to determine the speed and was driven by an attachment on the output shaft of the motor and mounted on a bracket fixed to the navigators table. The calliper arms were held inwards by a restraining system, retained by a bombslip. At the moment of release the safety pin was automatically removed. The height of release had to be 60 feet, at a speed of 240–250 mph, and it had to be released at between 400 and 500 yards from the dam wall.

The Upkeep casing was built at the Vickers works at Barrow-in-Furness and at Elswick and Walker on Tyneside. The HE-filled cylinders or casing was prepared at the Royal Ordnance Factory at Chorley, Lancashire and the inert or non-active cylinders in factories in Woolwich, south-east London.

At the same time as Upkeep, Operation Highball was being activated.

On 1 April 1943, 618 Squadron was formed at RAF Skitten, their role, to attack the German Fleet in Norway, which was to coincide with 617 Squadron's attack on the German dams. The weapon, similar to Upkeep, was named Highball and the target date 15 May 1943.

This special weapon was to be used by 618 Squadron operating with Mosquitoes, whereas 617 Squadron were to use Lancasters. Highball was much smaller than Upkeep. It was described as a special depth charge spun backwards at 1,000 rpm and released from the well of the fuselage to bounce on the water, when, on impact with the target it would rebound, and, still spinning, would curve underneath the ship and explode by the use of a hydrostatic pistol at a preselected depth. It weighed 1,289lbs, of which 600lb was Torpex charge.

It had three-eighths high quality steel and was fused with a modified hydrostatic pistol Mark IV and set to explode at 30 feet. The height of the drop was 60 feet and the speed at drop was 360 mph. Trials began at Manston in Kent with Squadron Leader Maurice 'Shorty' Longbottom, DFC, (killed 6 January 1945, aged 29) of Vickers Armstrong Ltd at Weybridge as the test pilot. He was assisted by Squadron Leader Charles Rose, DFC, DFM. A number of trials were carried out throughout April 1943 at Manston, also at Angle Bay, Milford Haven in South Wales. The case of the bomb was thickened to prevent buckling and five-eighth inch bolts substituted for half-inch bolts.

In May 1943 trials were moved to RAF Turnberry in Scotland. On 10 May, a full size steel clad weapon was released into Loch Striven. On 14 May, two Highball weapons were delivered to 618 Squadron, but by the end of May only fifteen had reached the squadron. On 17 May, a Mosquito, DZ 493, hit a vehicle on take-off, a lorry, van, and balloon cable burst into flames. The pilot, Wing Commander Hutchinson was only slightly injured. After further trials and tests at Turnberry they again reverted to Reculver, near Margate.

In August 1943 the whole thing was abandoned because the prime target, the German battleship *Tirpitz*, had moved to Kaa Fjord and was out of the range of UK based Mosquitoes.

In June 1944 Highball was considered for attacks on the Japanese Fleet in the Far East and 150 Highball weapons were taken there.

However, this never took place and 618 Squadron were disbanded in June 1945.

Of the 120 Upkeep bombs made, only nineteen were dropped in anger.

The cost of the bombs for Upkeep and Highball and the modifications to the Lancasters and Mosquitos was £411,895. In today's money this would be £14,000,000.

CHAPTER 3

The Preparation

The only aircraft suitable to carry a weapon which some called a bomb, or others a mine as did the operation record book for 617 Squadron, was the Lancaster bomber.

In 1936 the Air Ministry issued specifications P/13/36 and B/12/36. It was to be an aircraft that could alternate between long-range and very heavy bomb loads; when take-off would be made possible by catapult launching in an overloaded condition. It had to have high performance but at the same time be strong defensively. It would be a large aircraft but not exceed a span of 100 feet. It should also be able to retain height with one engine out of action and should have four engines.

Its performance:

Speed: At 15,000; not less than 230 mph.

Range: At normal loading at 15,000 feet; not less than 1,500 miles.

Crew: Six; two pilots, one to act as navigator, one flight engineer, one observer to act as front gunner, bomb aimer and relief W/T operator on long flights.

Armament: Two forward guns; each gun with not less than 600 rounds of ammunition.
Two mid-ship guns; each gun having 1,000 rounds of ammunition.
In the tail four guns; each having 1,000 rounds of ammunition.

The Lancaster was preceded by the ill-fated Manchester, both produced by Avro. In 1939 these aircraft became the design for the Ideal Bomber for the Royal Air Force. The Lancaster came into service in 1942 after the failure of the Manchester.

The crew consisted of a pilot who was the Captain, a flight engineer who looked after the engines and the petrol consumption of each engine; he also assisted the pilot on take-off. A wireless-operator who kept them in touch with base; the navigator who plotted their route; the bomb aimer who took over the aircraft on the bombing run; and last but not least, two air gunners whose task was to look after the aircraft, the mid-upper gunner was able to see enemy fighters coming in above and below, and the rear gunner, who faced the other way made sure a fighter did not attack from the rear.

In April 1943 Lancaster E.D. 825/G was sent to the Aircraft Armament Experimental Establishment at Boscombe Down, for modification to carry an item called a store – which would be the bouncing bomb.

The changes to a standard Lancaster were:

- Two guns fitted in the front turret.
- In the tail the usual four guns.
- Also at this stage a free ball-mounted gun, which later was removed.
- The bomb doors were removed and the fuselage modified on each side of the fuselage.
- The normal saucer-shaped transparent moulding, which carried the bomb aimer's window, was replaced by a hemispherical type window.
- A wireless transmitter aerial extended from the mast to each fin.

There were no barrage balloon cutters; the boxes for the cutters were sealed. There was no de-icing equipment; at such low heights this was not necessary.

The first type 464 Prevising Lancaster, ED 765-G, went to the Royal Aeronautical Establishment on 8 April 1943; the second of three, ED 817-G, went to RAF Manston on 20 April 1943 and the third, ED 825-G, to the A&AEE at Boscombe Down. Also on 8 April 1943,

First type 464 Prevising Lancaster

the first aircraft that was to be sent to 617 Squadron, ED 864-G;
arrived at RAF Scampton. The last of the twenty Lancasters did not
arrive until 13 May 1943. Needless to say this aircraft did not return
from the dams raid.

On the early modified Lancaster plans a belly-ventral gun was
shown, but later removed as not being suitable for low-level operations.

CHAPTER 4

X/617 Squadron is formed

On 15 March 1943, Air Vice-Marshal Ralph Cochrane, the AOC of 5 Group based at St Vincent's Hall, Grantham, Lincolnshire, was told by the Commander-in-Chief of Bomber Command, Sir Arthur Harris, of Upkeep and that he would like him to pick a squadron from his group to carry it out. Cochrane felt that forming a new squadron would be a better idea, but from men of 5 Group. They would be in the main, men with much experience and operations under their belt.

Harris then asked Cochrane who he thought should command the new squadron, without hesitation he said, 'Wing Commander Guy Gibson, DSO, DFC'. Gibson was only twenty-four and just about to finish his third tour, two with bombers and one on night fighters. Having been with 83 Squadron at the outbreak of war and then commanded 106 Squadron from 1942 to 1943, he was the ideal man. Being a regular airman he knew what he wanted and expected it to be done without question.

In March 1943, a WAAF, Morfydd Jane Brooks was posted in from Waddington, she was married and her husband was serving abroad. She remembers Gibson as being very particular about dress and appearance. The young WAAF's were told a new squadron was being formed for a very special operation and to keep quiet about anything they heard or saw. Her duties in the officer's mess was to lay out the tables for meals, the hours the aircrew worked was so erratic that a hot meal had always to be ready on their return. The explanation being, 'For They Were The Warriors'. This was how the aircrew were regarded at the time, and quite rightly so, as the air force was all about flying and the support to them vitally important. The young WAAF's also got used to the aircrew banter such as, 'How is your sex life?'

31

Gibson and four crew members.

Towards the end of their time at Syerston – Gibson and 'Nigger' with various aircrew

and 'Would you like to sleep with me?' This was all part of being a woman in those days in the services. It was taken in good heart by the WAAF's, who realized the job and danger the crews were facing each day, but many relationships were created on stations and much sadness when the crews did not return.

Gibson had expected to go on leave when Cochrane sent for him and asked him to do one more trip, but when he asked what sort of trip, he was told that he would find out at a later stage – this turned out to be much later. But he agreed and on 17 March 1943, 5 Group HQ received a letter from Bomber Command informing them of a special weapon with the codename Upkeep.

Wing Commander Wally Dunn, a regular airman who had served under Harris as a Corporal and while with him had perfected the method of crews speaking to each other in the aircraft, was sent for. At the time he was the Chief Signals Officer at 5 Group. Cochrane asked him to provide the new squadron, still unnamed, but for a while to be known as 'X', with radar and communications. It had now become a 'Churchill Priority' with a cover plan that it was an attack on the German battleship *Tirpitz*.

On 18 March 1943, Cochrane again met with Gibson. Present on this occasion was Group Captain Charles Whitworth, Station Commander, RAF Scampton, Lincolnshire, the station chosen to be the home of 'X' Squadron, as it was known until 24 March 1943, when it became 617 Squadron. On 21 March 1943 the men of the new squadron began to arrive. Meeting them was Flight Sergeant 'Chiefy' Powell, who was posted in from 57 Squadron, another squadron based at Scampton. Not known to many, George was an ex-air gunner before the war, but took his AG brevet off as he felt it would help him if the men coming in thought he was ground staff and not ex-aircrew, he had very little time to get the squadron up and running and did not want any familiarity to get in its way. Conditions at RAF Scampton were not good, with cramped quarters and a lack of facilities to cope with a new squadron.

Another who came from 57 Squadron was Sergeant Jim Heveron. He became the Orderly Room Sergeant and he and Powell scrounged paper, furniture and other things to set up some sort of orderly room. Jim had registered for military service in June 1939, he was then 20. As soon as war was declared he gave up his job and went to sign up as a fighter pilot. He was told the RAF did not need fighter pilots

Jim Heveron. © Mrs Heveron

as they already had plenty. But when he was asked what he did for a living and he told them 'statistician', as he had a BSc at London University, he was grabbed there and then as a clerk. He was sent to RAF Uxbridge and there he lived in a tent on the sports fields. Within three days and no training at all he was sent to France. He sailed from Southampton to Cherburg in France, to a small village north of Arras. His billet was a cow shed. In January 1940 he was posted to 57 Squadron, who were just outside Amiens. After being there for some time, a message came to pack up and evacuate within twelve hours.

The aircraft were to fly to an airfield on the French/Belgium border; and the ground staff were to proceed by train and road. All the spare aviation equipment was piled up in the middle of the airfield and set

Guy Gibson with Maltby in pre-dams discussions at RAF Scampton

alight, the Blenheim aircraft of 57 Squadron were raked with tracer bullets to prevent them and the fuel getting into the hands of the enemy. In the following days they were bombed and attacked from the air. On one occasion, as they were being driven along a French road, they were stopped by an army captain and told to draw up a rifle and fifty rounds of ammunition, but the RAF driver, a First World War chap, said they were all 'Sprogs' and had never fired a rifle, he then drove off before the captain could say anymore. When they reached the coast they managed to get on the *Monas Queen*, a peacetime cross-channel steamer. As they set sail Boulogne fell and the Germans reached the dock gates, so after a sleep he found himself back in Southampton. Jim stayed with 57 Squadron until he joined 617 Squadron in March 1943.

By the evening of 21 March, 250 airmen of all manner and trades had been booked in and accommodated. On 24 March 1943, 'X' Squadron became 617 Squadron and Gibson officially took over as commanding officer.

No. 2 Hangar at Scampton, previously used by 49 Squadron, had been cleaned out and ten Lancasters – eight of which were new – had arrived. The crews arrived between the period of 24 March 1943 and 17 April 1943, 147 men in all. Four pilots came from 57 Squadron, three from 97 Squadron, four from 50 Squadron, three from 106 Squadron (Gibson's old squadron), two from 49 Squadron, and one each from 44, 61, 207, and 467 Squadrons.

Gibson had just finished a tour with 106 Squadron, for which he was recommended and awarded a bar to his DSO. In the recommendation Harris wrote, 'Any captain who completes 272 sorties (173 Bomber and 99 Night fighter) in an outstanding manner is worth two DSO's, if not a Victoria Cross. The Victoria Cross of course, has to be awarded for one action and not a period of action. On reflection anyone who completes one operation, particularly in 1943/44, is worth a VC.'

The calibre of the pilots posted in was high; Flight Lieutenant Joe McCarthy RCAF, but born in the USA, had been a lifeguard in the USA; Flight Lieutenant Les Munro RNAF; and Squadron Leader David Maltby, were all from 97 Squadron. Joe was 23, a big man in every sense who had already been recommended for the DFC after thirty operations. Les was 24, had been a farmer in New Zealand and had been to Berlin three times, he had also been recommended for the DFC. Both DFCs were awarded at a later date. One of McCarthy's

Joe McCarthy and crew

crew, Sergeant George Johnson, was due to be married and at the initial interview with Gibson, McCarthy told him of this and Gibson gave George a forty-eight hour pass. George was married on 3 April 1943 in Torquay and back on duty on 5 April 1943. David Maltby was also 23 and from Sussex. He had already been awarded the DFC after twenty-seven operations in 1942 and had just returned to 97 Squadron when he was posted to 617 Squadron.

Flight Lieutenant Bill Astell also had a DFC from operations in Malta and North Africa. He also was 23. He had been shot down in the desert on 31 May 1942 when on an operation to attack Derna airfield. They dropped their first stick of bombs successfully, but on the second run were attacked by a ME 109 fighter and set on fire, Astell gave the order to bale out. He and another member of the crew, Pilot Officer Dodds, did not have time to bale out, so they crashed landed and set out across the desert. Pilot Officer Dodds became a PoW in Italy, but later escaped. Bill Astell arrived safely in Cairo.

Flying Officer Geoff Rice was a little older at 26, both he and Astell came from 57 Squadron, so they had not too far to travel.

Flight Lieutenant John Hopgood was 21, after thirty-two operations he was awarded the DFC, which had been recommended by Gibson as commanding officer of 106 Squadron. Flight Lieutenant David Shannon RAAF was only 20 and came from South Australia, where he had been a bank teller. He had been awarded the DFC after twenty-six operations. When he joined 617 Squadron at the end of March he had flown no less than thirty-six operations. One of his crew, Sergeant Jim Fraser from Canada, had married a girl from Doncaster.

There were two other Australians posted in. Flying Officer Les Knight, who came in on 26 March 1943 was 22 and came from Victoria, he also had been recommended for the DFC for completing twenty-six operations. Mick Martin was 25 and came from New South Wales. He began his career as a bomber pilot on Hampdens with 455 Squadron, before a posting to 50 Squadron in April 1942. On arrival with 617 Squadron he had completed thirty-six operations.

Flight Sergeant Bill Townsend, DFM, also came in on 26 March 1943, and was also 22. He had joined the Royal Artillery when war broke out and suffered greatly with air sickness, as did Hutchison, Gibson's radio operator. It was so bad that even after the war he could not look down in a car or train without feeling sick. He did not – as many did – have that great urge to fly, but somehow it seemed a better option than the army, so he volunteered for aircrew, but his airsickness nearly meant he failed. Somehow he got through and first started flying Hampden bombers, he was still under training and at

Les Knight and crew

Hay, Howard, Shannon, Leggo, Spafford, Martin and Kellow. © *Imperial War Museum*

McCarthy and Shannon, Woodhall Spa, 1944

OTU when the 1,000 bomber raid to Cologne took place and every available squadron and training unit was used. He also went on the second 1,000 raid to Essen, all before he had carried out a 'second dickie' trip – when you flew on operations with an experienced crew before getting your aircraft and crew. When he joined 49 Squadron they were using the ill-fated Manchester before converting to Lancasters. He had twenty-eight operations under his belt when asked if he would like to join a new squadron for 'special duties'

Flight Sergeant Cyril Anderson also came from 49 Squadron and had flown twenty-two operations. He hailed from Wakefield in Yorkshire and started the war as ground crew before training as a pilot in Canada and joining 49 Squadron in February 1943.

At the end of March 1943 three Canadians joined 617 Squadron. Flight Sergeant Ken Brown came from Moose Jaw, Saskatchewan; he was 23 and had flown just seven operations with 44 Squadron when he arrived. Sergeant Vernon Byers (later Pilot Officer) also came from Saskatchewan, a place called Star City, but at 32 much older than the average aircrew. He came from 467 Squadron where he had completed only five operations. Pilot Officer Lewis Burpee was 25 and had graduated with a BA Degree in English from Queen's University, Kingston, Ontario. He loved music, obviously getting it from his mother Lillian who was a member of the Ottawa Symphony Orchestra. His father, also named Lewis, had served in the Field Ambulance of the Canadian Medical Corps in Europe in the First World War. He had arrived in the UK in September 1941, although he wanted to be a fighter pilot, he found himself flying Whitley bombers. In 1942 he married an English girl named Lillian – the same name as his mother – who had been evacuated from London, shortly after, he was posted to Gibson's old squadron at Newark. After flying twenty-six operations he was awarded the DFM, in his recommendation it mentioned that he had been to Milan in daylight and had twice flown back to base with his aircraft shot up. In March 1943 he was commissioned a Pilot Officer when posted to 617 Squadron and his wife was expecting a child. His cousin Matthew Burpee had been killed in action in July 1941, while taking part in a raid on Rotterdam.

Gibson formed a new crew, apart that is from wireless operator Flight Lieutenant Bob Hutchison, whom he brought with him from 106 Squadron. In the film, which will be dealt with later, the impression was given that his whole crew came with him.

Burpee and crew. © *Imperial War Museum*

Peterson, Anderson, Bickle, Buck, Green and Nugent. They returned from the Dams but were killed later. © *Mrs C. Anderson*

Left to right; Hewitt, Walker and Hutchison.106 Squadron, early 1942

A situation occurred when thirty of the ground crew, having come from living in Nissan huts and tents in open fields, found themselves in brick buildings and hangars to service the aircraft, but because of their previous situation their dress and uniforms were not acceptable to the RAF Police on the station. This resulted in men being put on charges and was brought to the attention of Gibson. He sent for George Powell, who explained the conditions the men had been in previously. Gibson then rang the clothing officer in the stores, who in all the services are always reluctant to part with any kit, at first he was not co-operative, but with a few well-chosen words from Gibson, his attitude soon changed. A special clothing parade was arranged for the next day, but before this took place Gibson had all the ground crew paraded in front him and told them that those that had been on a charge could forget it. However, once the clothing items had been replaced he expected and demanded a high standard of turn out. He was a regular officer and had been brought up on airmen looking like airmen. He also told them that security was at a premium and whatever they saw or heard they did not speak about at the local pub etc. He also said that if they were invited to go on trial flights by the crew he would encourage them to go, but to let someone know they had gone, if they did so, there was no need to put their name in the flight authorization book.

Towards the end of March he assembled the aircrew who had arrived in front of a hangar, he then stood on the bonnet of his car and told them that the odds were heavily against them on the upcoming operation and that anyone who wished to withdraw could do so without any question of being given the stigma of LMF (Lack of Morale Fibre), or to be completely correct, Losing the Confidence Of One's Commanding Officer. There were no withdrawals.

By his actions, Gibson showed he was in charge and prepared to back his men as long it was justified. The way Gibson commanded and wanted things done came over when, on one occasion, he told Jim Heveron that he was going to Group and to leave his flying helmet out for him to pick up later for a night-time training run. Jim in turn gave an order that Gibson's office was to be left open, but when Gibson later arrived he found the door locked. The airman, who had not left the office open as requested, had to break the glass above the door, climb in and get the flying helmet.

On 24 March 1943, 'Mutt' Summers drove down to Surhill, Wallis' drawing office. He had Gibson with him, who met Wallis for the first time. When asked if he had been told the target, Gibson replied that he had not the slightest idea. It would appear the list of people who were allowed to know the target did not include Gibson!

The codenames selected for the operation were:

Highball: The special weapon, a smaller version of the dams bomb.

Upkeep: The special weapon, as used on the attack on the dams.

Chastise: The operation against the dams.

To complete the orderly room and administration staff, Flight Lieutenant Harry Humphries arrived from 50 Squadron and replaced the previous Adjutant, who was not thought to be suitable. Squadron Leader Clifford Caple came in from Group HQ as Engineering Officer, Flight Lieutenant Henry Watson from 83 Squadron as Armament Officer and finally Flying Officer Malcolm Arthurton as the Medical Officer. All four men would have their work cut out in the coming weeks. Gibson's office was in No. 2 Hangar.

Rumours were already going round, with such an array of highly decorated crew members this was to be expected. In total seventeen DFC's, three bars to the DFC, three DSO's and ten DFM's. Attacks on the *Tirpitz,* which became the official cover plan to a mission to kidnap Hitler – were rife.

Flight Lieutenant Barlow, DFC, and his crew did not arrive until 7 April 1943 and found things pretty chaotic at Scampton. Twice during his tour he had come back on three engines, Stuttgart in November 1942, and Berlin on 1 March 1943. He had also brought back damaged aircraft from Turin and on another Berlin trip. At 32 he was much older than many of the pilots.

Squadron Leader Henry Maudslay, DFC, who was to be flight commander of B Flight at 617 Squadron, arrived on 31 March 1943. His DFC was awarded in 1941 after a successful tour with 44 Squadron flying Hampdens. He had not long been posted to 50 Squadron when the call to 617 Squadron came. He was 'B' Flight Commander. His team was: Navigation Officer: Flying Officer R.A. Urquhart, DFC, RCAF, Bombing Leader: Flying Officer E.C. Johnson, Gunnery Leader: Flying Officer W.J. Tytherleigh, DFC.

Air Vice-Marshal John Slesser – when AOC of 5 Group – wrote that Maudslay was one of his most outstanding captains.

On 6 April 1943, Pilot Officer Warner Ottley arrived from 207 Squadron. He had completed a tour of thirty-one operations with 207 Squadron and had one more to do with 617 Squadron.

On 10 April 1943 the final three pilots came from 57 Squadron, they were Flight Sergeant William Divall, Squadron Leader Henry Young and Flight Lieutenant Harold Wilson. Divall was 22 and had only been with the squadron since February when the call came for 617 Squadron. In this case the theory that all the pilots and crews were highly experienced is exposed, but as he did not actually take part in the raid, may well mean that there was an element of reserve crews being made available.

Henry Young was aged 26, although in the RAF, he was an American. He had been to Oxford and rowed as No. 2 in the last Oxford boat race in 1939 before the start of the war. He and his crew won the race by two lengths in twenty and half minutes, which meant they were certainly moving. He completed a tour of operations with 102 Squadron and was awarded the DFC. On two occasions he had to ditch in the sea, after the second ditching he seemed to inherit the nickname 'Dinghy'. There is also a story related by the late Wing Commander Wally Dunn, 5 Group's Signals officer, 'One day his flight pilots came to see me as Station Signal Officer and asked if

'Dinghy' Young (second from back) taking part in the Oxford Crew Boat Race, 2nd April, 1938

'Dinghy' Young (on right), pre-1938

Squadron Leader H.M. Young DFC and Bar, March 1942. © Roy Chappell

I would teleprint a signal from, HQ Bomber Command to RAF Driffield, posting Flight Lieutenant H.M. Young to command a new dinghy training school at Calshot. Following a custom of mine to do anything for my aircrew I duly typed it out and stamped it with various signal marks, and put it out with the signals for the day. It worked very well, to the extent that 'Dinghy' bought everybody a drink in the mess before the truth was known.' So how he became 'Dinghy' is debateable. His second tour was with 104 Squadron, including a period in the Middle East, when in June 1942 his squadron was sent to Malta. After flying fifty-one operations he was awarded a bar to his DFC. He was 'A' Flight Commander. His team was: Navigation Officer; Flying Officer R. MacFarlane, Bombing Leader; Pilot Officer J. Fort, Gunnery Leader; Flying Officer H.S. Glinz RCAF.

Gibson's crew did not arrive together, but one after the other, the Navigator was Flight Lieutenant Torger Taerum from Canada, he had completed a tour with 50 Squadron and came to 617 Squadron from 1654 Conversion Unit at Wigsley. His Flight Engineer was Sergeant John Pulford, who had only flown ten operations with 97 Squadron, but had obviously created a good impression to be in Gibson's crew and had arrived on 4 April. The Wireless Operator was Flight Lieutenant Robert (Bob) (Hutch) Hutchison, DFC, he had been awarded his DFC with 106 Squadron, Gibson's previous squadron and was the only one from his previous crew to go with him to 617 (Not as the film, which gave the impression they all went). He always kept the curtain closed in his wireless cabin and so never saw the flak coming up. He was also airsick on every flight but never failed to do his job.

Flying Officer Frederick 'Spam' Spafford, DFM, Gibson's bomb aimer, was from Adelaide, Western Australia. On his first tour with 50 Squadron he was awarded an immediate DFM after only fifteen operations and ended up flying thirty-one operations. He was commissioned in January 1943. His rear gunner, Flight Lieutenant Richard (Trev) Trevor-Roper, DFM, had joined the RAF after transferring from the army, where he had served with the Royal Artillery. He had also flown as an air gunner in the crew of Air Vice-Marshal Sir Gus Walker, when he commanded 50 Squadron, Trevor-Roper completed his tour in 1941. After a spell of rest he returned to 50 Squadron and by the time he was posted to 617 Squadron he had completed thirty-five operations for his second tour, which took his total to fifty-one.

The final member of his crew was the front gunner, Flight Sergeant George Deering, RCAF; he had been born in Ireland. He had also completed a tour of thirty-five operations. His commission to Pilot Officer came through the day after the dams operation.

Gibson's Team Leaders were: Bombing Leader; Flight Lieutenant R.C. Hay, DFC, RAAF, Signals Leader; Flight Lieutenant R.E.G. Hutchison, DFC, Gunnery Leader; Flight Lieutenant R.D. Trevor-Roper, DFM, Navigation Leader; Flight Lieutenant J.F. Leggo, DFC, RAAF.

One who arrived early in March 1943 was Flight Sergeant James (Jim) Clay, he was to be Flight Lieutenant Les Munro's bomb aimer. He had six brothers, all serving in the Army, Navy, and Merchant Navy, a sister working in a factory and his father in the Home Guard, so from one family nine people were serving their country in one way or another. Jim had completed a tour with 97 Squadron and with all his family serving he thought it only right that he continue.

Left to right; Bill Howarth, John Pulford, Percy Pigeon, Harvey Weeks

The officers' mess at Scampton was shared with 57 Squadron and over the weeks there was many a crack about the fact that 617 Squadron were not flying on operations. Flying Officer Dave Rodger from Canada, who was down to fly with Joe McCarthy, was amazed to see so many decorated airmen in one room.

Dave Rodger, McCarthy's rear gunner during the Dams raid

Back row left to right; Onacia, Sutherland, O'Brien, Brown, Weeks, Thrasher, Deering, Radcliffe, McLean, McCarthy, McDonald. Front row left to right; Pigeon, Taerum, Walker, Gowrie, Rodger

RAF Scampton had a full background. It was just north of Lincoln and was known in the First World War as RAF Brattleby. It opened in 1916 with wooden huts and six hangars. In 1935 work commenced with C Type hangars, brick barrack blocks, workshops and messes. In 1936 it became part of No. 3 Group Bomber Command, but in 1939 transferred to No. 5 Group. It was from here that Guy Gibson flew operationally with 83 Squadron, flying Handley Page Hampdens.

In January 1943 it became No. 52 Base, 5 Group, but still had grass runways, not ideal for four-engined bombers. Nevertheless, in March 1943, 617 Squadron was formed here. They remained until August 1943 when they moved to RAF Coningsby. It then closed for a while, concrete runways were installed, and did not open again until July 1944.

Today it's the home of the famous Red Arrows Display Team. The RAF Scampton museum is housed in one of the wartime hangars. Here there are over 400 artefacts, including many from the Dambuster period. It can be visited, but only by contact ahead, as it is not always manned, and with security on entry to an RAF Station being strict, it is not possible to obtain access without prior notice.

The Victoria Cross.
© *Mike King*

DSO © *Mike King*

DFC © *Mike King*

CGM © *Mike King*

DFM © *Mike King*

CHAPTER 5

Training

The training for the dams raid began on 31 March 1943 and would continue for forty-two days and nights. This involved mainly low-level cross-country flights to get used to flying at extreme low heights which prior to this, for bomber crews, would have been frowned upon. People like Mick Martin had been low flying for some while, at that time against regulations, but now it was legal and the reason he and others were selected to fly with 617 Squadron. The bomb aimers on Lancasters soon became used to foliage close to their noses, below the nose of the aircraft. The entries in Squadron Leader Maudslay's navigator, Flying Officer Robert Urquhart's log-book on 31 March 1943 read: 'X-country 500 feet; low-level bombing speed 240 mph – 100 feet.'

At the end of the first week, twenty-six cross-country flights and 240 bombs had been dropped (conventional type), with an average error margin being 40 yards.

At this stage flights were flown in daylight. Night flying was expected to start around 10 April, the time estimated to be suitable for moonlight conditions that would be found in mid-May, the estimated time of the operation.

Lewis Burpee's navigator, Sergeant Tom Jaye, entered in his log-book for 1 April 'Low-level X-country and bombing,' this was repeated on the third and fourth, adding 'air-firing' on 4 April, when the air gunners practised gunnery from low-level. The area chosen for these flights was over and around lakes in North Wales.

Sergeant Richard Bolitho, who was to fly as rear gunner with Flight Lieutenant Astell in 'B' Baker, came from Ireland and had joined the RAF in 1940. On his last leave Richard, Pilot Officer Floyd Wile, Warrant Officer Albert Garshowitz, both from Canada and Sergeant

John Kinnear from Scotland, had all been to Kimberley in Northern Ireland, the home of Richard's aunt. He had also recorded intense flying at low-level.

One problem among many was flying over water at night and how to judge the correct height of the aircraft above the surface. Ben Lockspeiser, knighted in 1946, and Director of Scientific Research at the Ministry of Aircraft Production, was asked for his help to try and solve this problem. He came up with using two spotlights, one under the tail and one in the nose of the Lancaster. They were set at pre-determined angles to cast a spotlight on the surface of the water. As the aircraft reduced height, so the two spots of light met, and when they did it meant they were at the correct height. This was first used in the First World War but met with problems and was not used again. In the Second World War it was used for anti-submarine warfare by the Royal Aircraft establishment. It was not a success in a choppy sea as it was impossible to identify when the lights actually met, however, over smooth water such as lakes there was a good chance it would work. Lockspeiser visited Cochrane with the idea and he agreed to have a Lancaster fitted with two spotlights at Farnborough. Trials were carried out over Lake Windermere which were a great success and the problem of flying over water at night at low-level was solved.

On 5 April 1943, Corporal Maurice Statham was serving as a motor transport driver in 5 Group HQ, as personal driver to the Air Officer Commanding Air Vice-Marshal Ralph Cochrane. He was detailed by Cochrane's personal secretary, Station Officer Carol Durant, to drive the AOC to RAF Scampton, collect Wing Commander Gibson and take him to 5 Group HQ at Grantham. Here, Gibson was told the target for the first time. Now that he knew the target he was told to practise low-level flying over various selected reservoirs in preparation for the operation.

In Gibson's log, which is now at the National Archives, there is an entry for 4 April: 'Lake near Sheffield' (probably Derwent) and for 5 April 1943: 'Scotland X-Country, Lakes.'

Pilot Officer Lance Howard, Sergeant Townsend's Australian navigator, remembered how hard it was flying at 60 feet, and the bouncing about incurred, due to Townsend not being able to use the automatic pilot. The weather was warm and the up-currents made the aircraft shake all over the sky. Despite this, Townsend was an excellent natural pilot and coped magnificently. Lance had trained as a pilot, but because of landing difficulties in an Anson he re-mustered as a navigator and served with 49 Squadron. Leading Aircraftman Keith 'lofty' Stretch remembers ground crews being able to hitch rides on the training flights, that is apart from exercises that were on the secret list, men were encouraged to go on the training flights. He was able to fly with Flying Officer Les Knight and found hedge-hopping a great thrill, and admired his skill and his calmness in doing so.

If the mission was to be a success, good air-to-air radio transmission, at heights from 50 to 1,000 feet, was vital. The first test of the TR 1196 radio transmitter fitted was on the 28 March, in daylight and carried out at a height of 2,600 feet on 5005 kcs R/T; a communication of 40 miles range was obtained. Further tests took place on 7 April between two aircraft, from 500 feet up to 15,000 feet, with an average range of 30 miles.

In one of the aircraft was Gibson and Wing Commander Wally Dunn, the 5 Group Chief Signals Officer, who was the most experienced man for the job. The results were quite good, but to be certain a night test had to be carried out. This proved to be hopeless, owing to continental waves and the background noise which occurred at night.

The week ending 15 April 1943 was a week of good weather and many of the problems were ironed out.

Flight Sergeant Lovell arrived from 57 Squadron, but was soon replaced by Flight Sergeant Divall, also from 57 Squadron. Pilot Officer Warner Ottley joined on 6 April 1943, about the same time as 'Dingy' Young, Anderson, and Flight Lieutenant Wilson.

The crews were out every day from the 9/15 April 1943. On 16 April, when walking back to the flight huts, the ground crew heard a loud noise, louder than usual, and when they looked back they saw not just one Lancaster taking off, but three in formation, then another three, again in formation. They spanned the whole of the grass runway before lifting off, then skimmed the hedges before making a slow bank to the left and disappearing for a few minutes. They then formed up and flew over the field at 200 feet, the ground crews then thought they have lost it and had gone mad.

There were of course complaints from farmers etc. in the area; they said that the cows were not providing milk and the chickens not laying eggs. Another said that motorists were ducking as the black painted four-engined Lancasters thundered past only 150 feet up. It is said that Group HQ, when replying to complaints such as this said, 'Our pilots have now been instructed to show due regard for other road-users.'

It was mainly the vibrations that caused the most problems to locals, causing roof tiles to come off; some thought the aircrew were joyriding. Some of the areas for training were Derwent Reservoir, Lake Bala, and the Vyrnwy and Elan Valleys. Today at Derwent is a memorial which reads: 'They paid for our freedom.'

The low flying expert Mick Martin was always on hand to give advice over the intercom as they dodged pylons, treetops and power lines in the dark.

In Joe McCarthy's crew they had quite a scare when flying at 30 feet – Les Munro flew underneath them.

On 11 April 1943, Gibson, with Bob Hay, DFC, the Bombing Leader who flew with Martin, flew down to Manston in a Miles Magister aircraft to see the first test of the Upkeep bomb being dropped. Bob had a lot of experience with 455 and 50 Squadrons and had been awarded the DFC after thirty-four operations.

The drop was at Reculver Bay, near Manston. The pilot, Sam Browne, travelling at a speed of 270 mph, was instructed by Wallis to give the bomb a backspin of 300 rpm and to let the mine go at 150 feet. But as the two aircraft approached, one carrying the cine camera to record the drop and the other carrying the bomb, Wallis realized that according to the white marker buoys, which were placed some yards offshore, the bomb carrying aircraft was too high. The bomb came away from the aircraft but instead of bouncing on the water it immediately sank out of sight.

On the return to Scampton, Gibson had engine failure when 300 feet above Margate. He once wrote that if you have an engine stop in a four engine aircraft you don't have to worry too much, but when it happens in a single engine aircraft there is only one way and that's down. The area in Thanet was filled with anti-aircraft landing obstacles but he managed to crash-land in a field and both he and Hay climbed out, shaken but unhurt. The aircraft was recovered a few days later by an RAF rescue unit from Manston.

A second test followed on 18 April 1943 with the aircraft flying much lower. Although the bomb did not sink, it did disintegrate in a shower of wood, steel bands and bolts, the heavy steel cylinder burst out with such force that one wooden segment smashed into the

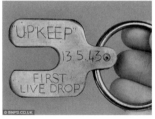

DFC belonging to Squadron Leader Maurice Longbottom and the bomb release key from the first live drop. © *Dominic Winter Auctions*

Lancaster's elevator as it passed over, jamming it. 'Mutt' Summers, the pilot on this second test, had a serious problem in maintaining height both then and later when landing. Back at Scampton, 617 Squadron continued training from 26 March to 22 April 1943. Map-reading at night at a height of 150 feet over water, was mainly the responsibility of the bomb aimer, who would lie in the nose of the aircraft. The bomb aimer also assisted the pilot in watching ahead when flying at low-level, keeping a sharp lookout for power lines, trees, tall chimneys and so on. He needed that assistance when flying fast and low, a short glance at his instruments could mean hitting or not hitting an obstacle ahead.

The track was previously calculated and drawn from forecast wind speed and direction. Both gunners would take drifts from time to time from the turrets, plus the bomb aimer through the bomb sight. These drift calculations enabled the navigator to adjust course as necessary. The bomb aimer endeavoured to give pinpoint positions mainly by visual sightings over land, and drifts calculated from flame floats dropped over water. A shortage of these was overcome by the SASO at 5 Group, who made 500 available to the squadron so they could operate through the moon period and on to the end of the month. They were fortunate that over the whole period of the training flights the weather was good.

Gibson's log book for the 16 April 1943 reads: 'Cornish X-Country at low-level with dummy attacks on lakes.'

Films on map-reading were shown at this time for all navigators and bomb aimers.

Daytime bombing from 100 feet by day and 150 feet by night continued at Wainfleet Sands Bombing Range. The speed had now been stressed by Wallis as 240 mph for the speed of release. Between the 16/22 April 1943; 179 bombs were dropped. At this stage Wallis had set the height as 150 feet, but he had determined the height for the drop of Upkeep was 60 feet. This was introduced to the crews on 26 April and also a new air speed of 210 mph. Although not known at this time, the raid was only three weeks away.

Flying a Lancaster bomber with a wing span of 102 feet, at night at a height of 60 feet, was extremely dangerous. The spotlights were adjusted to the new height of 60 feet from the previous 150 feet. The positioning of the spotlights was decided by three factors:

1. To simulate training at 150 feet.
2. To prevent oil smearing over the rear spotlight.
3. To shield the light as much as possible.

Two of the Lancasters were fitted with Synthetic Flying Equipment. This was also known as the Two Stage Blue Day-Night Flying System, invented by two brothers early in the war, Squadron Leaders Arthur and Charles Wood. Arthur had been a fighter pilot in the First World War, and both he and his brother saw service with the Technical Branch in the Second World War. Charles had a photographic business prior to the war and from 1940 to 1946. He received the MBE for his work on daytime flying systems.

The major problem in training for the dams raid was how to complete its training for an operation in full moonlight conditions, when the full moon periods only came monthly, over the period of the training there were only a few nights of ideal brightness. The Wood brothers solved this by creating moonlight conditions but flying during day time. This was achieved by the use of light-absorption filters – or colour filters – that could either cut off or produce different colours of the spectrum. A blue filter, for example, allowed the eye to see only the blue and green wavelengths of light, cutting off the yellow and red, whereas it's complementary amber filter cuts off the blue and the green, allowing only vision of the yellow and red. Together, this produced a complete blackout. In the Day-Night Flying System, all the windows of an aeroplane's cockpit were covered with a blue filter component, whilst pilot, navigator and bomb aimer wore goggles with amber-coloured glass. The effect was that all three men saw everything in the inside of the aircraft controls, instruments, maps etc., all in a subdued reddish light, exactly as one would expect to have at night in operational flying, whilst their vision through the blue windows simulated a dark or moonlit night. Gibson approached Charles Wood and eventually he had five aircraft fitted out with the system for use by his squadron.

The first arrived on 15 April 1943; the other four by the end of the month. With these aircraft, crews were able to train for some six weeks on intensive low-level training at any time of the day, flying as though in perfect moonlit conditions. Much of this training with the system was carried out over the water, at the Derwent Valley Reservoir in Derbyshire, which in many ways resembles the Mohne Dams in Germany. From 5 May 1943, training started on a reservoir four miles south of Uppingham. The Lancasters were delivered to 617 Squadron by ATA pilots.

Mr White of Huddersfield, Yorkshire, who was employed by A.V. Roe Ltd as an instrument fitter, remembered the fitting of the system. In April, he was called into the office of Phil Lightfoot, the man in charge of company activities at RAF Waddington; he was told that the work he was currently working on was to come to a halt and room made for a Lancaster coming from Scampton. Mr White was required to carry out urgent modifications involving a parcel which had already arrived and was lying on the floor of the hangar, to help him with this he was given three men.

When the Lancaster arrived it caused raised eyebrows as it did not have bomb doors and had a special release gear plus two extra landing lights fore and aft. All seemed a little odd with the task ahead of them.

This task consisted of covering the windscreen, canopy and side windows of the cockpit, with removable Perspex panels which had arrived the day after the aircraft. Although precise measurements were shown on a drawing, brown paper was used to make templates from which the panels were cut to size. This was necessary owing to slight variations during fabrication of the cockpit and could not be avoided, thus every Lancaster's window panel could vary slightly from one to the next. The male half of a dot fastener was affixed to the cut-out, window frames and panels were given a trial fit and each fastener point marked off. The completed panels were given to the WAAF workshop, where black linen hems were machined on and then the female half of the fasteners were fitted to the hems. The panels were then fastened into position and after inspection the Lancaster was taken out onto the tarmac for a vibration test with engines roaring at full throttle.

On the morning the job was completed Phil Lightfoot told Mr White that a Wing Commander Gibson would be arriving to inspect the job and he was to make any alterations the Wing Commander might require. When he arrived Gibson climbed into the Lancaster exchanging a few formal words. Inside, White decided not to make any comments, but to let the Wing Commander make a thorough inspection and decide for himself if he was happy or not. Gibson sat in the pilot's seat and tried on one or two pairs of goggles, at the same time examining the instrument panel in front of him. After he had finished, White asked him if he was satisfied, he was, and said everything seemed OK.

With all this work and odd looking aircraft, security was of the highest. Each new arrival was issued with a pass which included fingerprints and a photograph of the person. All personnel were instructed not to refer to their work, if they did they would be put under arrest immediately.

The conversion to the three aircraft at Waddington took fourteen days. Working in the cramped cockpit around the controls and the control column took much longer than if it had been in a more open area. The main concern was to avoid bulges and tension in the Perspex on take-off, when vibration would spring the fasteners apart.

At Wainfleet bombing range two screens had been erected 750 feet apart; this was for simulation of the actual attack. However a gale on 26 April 1943 blew them away. The attack area was changed to Uppingham, so although more screens were built they were not used again.

On top of the dam there were canvas screens 200 × 12 feet, to simulate the towers on the Mohne Dam. Exercises went ahead from 23 to 27 April 1943.

During this time Wallis had his own problems. Dropping the bomb from 150 feet, the casing – despite having been strengthened – broke up or sunk on contact with the water. He met Gibson on 24 April 1943 and told him that the only way to solve the problem was to release the bomb from 60 feet at 232 mph.

Another problem being worked on was – at what distance from the dam wall should the bomb be dropped? A special rangefinder sight was devised, constructed and fitted to the aircraft. This came from Wing Commander Leslie Dann, a regular RAF officer (later Air Commander, CBE) who retired in 1957 and died in 1965. The idea was a simple triangle of plywood with an eyehole as a backsight and a nail on each arm of the triangle. One looked through the eyehole and lined up the two towers on the dam with the nails on the sight, when the towers corresponded to the two nails the aircraft was at the point of release.

There were others who found their own way of locating the distance needed for the drop. Len Sumpter, flying as bomb aimer with David Shannon, found that using the wooden device at low heights and with turbulence made it difficult to hold the sight steady, so he put two blue markers on the clear-vision panel and attached the string to the screens each side of the panel. Lying down flat in the nose of the aircraft he drew the string back to his nose.

Yet another problem associated with low flying exercises was air sickness. The Squadron Medical Officer, Flying Officer Atherton, took to flying on exercises to attempt to find a remedy. On 25 April 1943 he flew with Maudslay in Lancaster ED 906 over the Derwent water. In his logbook Maudslay wrote, 'Low flying, weather bumpy – everybody airsick after half an hour. Total flying time one hour.'

The lowering of the height to 60 feet also caused problems with damage to aircraft. Squadron Leader Maudslay came back with his Lancaster so badly damaged, many marvelled that he had got back at all. Airframe fitters spent many hours replacing the damaged panels.

Time was now getting short, with the high water period on the Mohne Dam and a moonlight night only weeks away.

On 28 April 1943, a Highball was dropped from a Mosquito from 130 feet, at 350 mph, into a headwind of 15 mph, revs 700 per minute. It bounced four or five times, travelled 1,000 yards and although dented, it suffered no major damage. A further drop the next day also had the same effect. On the same day, Upkeep was tested encased in ash wood. It was dropped from 60 feet, at 258 mph into a 5 mph headwind and revolving at 500 revolutions per minute, it bounced four or five times and covered 600–700 yards. This resulted in the sub-committee giving the go-ahead for Operation Chastise to commence straight away. It also meant that if this did not proceed it would be 1944 before the opportunity would come again.

At the end of April the modified Lancasters began to arrive. On 22 April 1943, ED 887 arrived for Young, ED 865 for Burpee and ED 864 for Astell. On 23 April 1943, ED 909 arrived for Martin, ED 886 for Townsend and ED 906 for Maltby. On 28 April 1943, ED 910 arrived for Ottley.

In early May, much training took place with the spotlights over all types of water, making dummy runs over the Eyebrook Reservoir, often known as the Uppingham Lake, until all the crews were familiar with its use.

A further five Lancasters arrived at this time: ED 953 for Gibson, ED 925 for Hopgood, ED 921 for Munro, ED 918 for Brown, ED 929 for Shannon, and finally ED 924 for Anderson. They were put into service immediately. The crews spent a great deal of time fitting out their aircraft with any small gadgets that they felt were needed. One of these which proved of the greatest use was an additional altimeter; this took the place of the usual visual loop direction indicator which enabled the pilot to fly at night without having to lower his eyes from the horizon ahead of him. This was mentioned early on in low flight training, when a lowering of the eyes could have serious consequences.

On 4 May 1943, Wing Commander Wally Dunn, said he felt VHF was the only answer to the communications problem. Using the previous methods was again tried out but found to be useless. The only solution was to use a TR 1143 transmitter as used in fighters, and never used in bombers previously. The previous transmitter had been TR 1196. With the help of RAE and Wing Commander Allerston of HQ Bomber Command, it was arranged for Flight Lieutenant Bone to assist. It was he who suggested the use of the TR 1143 and it was the RAE Radio Department who prototyped the installation and No. 26 (Signals) Group provided the manpower. On 7 May, a RAE representative, plus an officer and twenty-five men from the Signals Group had arrived. And by 1730 hours on 9 May 1943 all eighteen aircraft had been fitted with the new transmitter. On the evening of 9 May 1943 a further test was set up with Squadron Leader Maudslay, flying a course of 180 degrees at 500 feet and Squadron Leader Young circling Scampton at 500 feet. Communications were to be made and held to an extreme range, then Young would make flat turns around Scampton and indicate the course over 10 degrees by radio transmitter, so that the observer flying with Maudslay could make an estimation of the polar diagram to be expected. The test showed no blind spots and the communication was good. By 11 May 1943 all modifications had been made on all aircraft. On the same day, Gibson and Martin tested a modified aircraft on an Upkeep drop from 50 feet, this was so low that damage was caused to the aircraft elevators and it was then decided to raise the height to 60 feet.

To save flying time the squadron pilots practised with the new VHF radios on the ground. They were wired up in the crew room and an inter-communications system, including twenty sockets wired in a common circuit set up, these ran through both flight commanders' offices and around the crew room. Each pilot plugged into a socket and by means of A1134A amplifier, the entire R/T procedure was practised.

At Scampton thirty-seven bombs were delivered and nineteen to Manston. None of the bombs at this stage had their explosive content. Also delivered to Scampton was a Coles crane, six modified bomb trolleys, two mobile gantries, three sets of lifting tackle and twenty winches. Instruction was given that no attempt should be made to fit the bombs to the Lancasters. The Armaments Officer, Pilot Officer Watson, had been attached to Manston, but on the 1 May returned to Scampton and would be in charge of loading the bombs. All the bombs were locked away out of sight to avoid any further speculation. When the Lancasters arrived without a top gun turret, a lack of bomb doors and the strange looking bomb bay, they caused much speculation as to what was going on.

During the loading of the bombs there was a panic when one of the bombs fell as it was being winched up to the aircraft, following a fault in the release system. Mick Martin sped off to find the armaments officer, but when he arrived back the panic was already over and he declared the mine 'safe'.

The motor to enable the bomb to spin was a VSG engine, very compact, 15 to 18 inches in height and hydraulically driven by a pump from one of the inboard engines, the same sort of system that operated the flaps and undercarriage.

For the bomb aimer, stirrups had been fitted to the front gun turret so that the air gunner's legs could be kept out of the way of the bomb aimer below him. It was reported that the front gunner would be the smallest of the two air gunners in the crew. The air gunners had decided between them that to give maximum 'scare effect' every round would be a tracer round.

On 5 May 1943, Gibson received the aircraft he was to use on the raid, ED 932-G and made a flight, testing out the spotlights at 60 feet. On 7 May 1943 all leave was cancelled or stopped. On 10 May 1943 a letter was sent to Harris from Air Commodore S. Bufton, Director Bomber Operations, it contained the following: 'I am directed to inform you that in order to avoid specific mention of the Mohne, Eder and Sorpe Dams, in future correspondence and discussion, it has been decided that these dams should be called by the following:

Mohne Dam: Objective 'X'
Eder Dam: Objective 'Y'
Sorpe Dam: Objective 'Z'

On 13 May 1943, further sorties were carried out by the Photo Reconnaissance Unit (PRU) at Benson to cover the Eder and Sorpe Dams. This was to check that further defences had not been put in place.

Also on 13 May 1943 was the first dropping of the armed, and loaded with a Torpex, Upkeep bomb, the aircraft was flown by Squadron Leader Maurice 'Shorty' Longbottom, DFC, Gibson was aboard the aircraft to observe the results of the drop, also aboard was Group Captain Whitworth, the Station Commander at RAF Scampton. Maudslay, in his aircraft, had the Squadron Medical Officer Malcolm

Arthurton, who recorded 'Experiment taking Chloretone for airsickness; result – no nausea or airsickness among the crew. Flying time four hours.' He had recorded flying in ED 906, but in fact it was ED 937-Z, the last modified aircraft to arrive on the squadron. The third aircraft was flown by David Shannon and the rehearsal proved to be a complete success.

On 14 May 1943 a further sortie was made on the Mohne Dam from Benson

Flying Officer Malcolm Arthurton, Medical Officer 617 Squadron 1943.

Reculver

but failed to cover the dam itself. However, it did show that the water in the valley had risen and was only about six feet below the top of the Dam.

A full rehearsal was also carried out at 2200 hours on the 14 May at the Abberton Reservoir, five miles south-west of Colchester, which was about the time they would be airborne on the night of the operation. The reservoir was built in 1939 and situated near the village of Layer de La Haye. The other reservoir was at Eyebrook, near Corby in Northamptonshire, which was built between 1937 and 1940. Today it is a fishing sanctuary popular with anglers and birdwatchers.

On 15 May 1943, a final photograph sortie was made. This was successful and a report was drafted by Flying Officer d'Arcy Smith during the night of the 15/16 May 1943 and issued early on 16 May 1943. Having read this report the Air Officer Commanding of 5 Group, Ralph Cochrane, gave the order that the operation would take place on 16/17 May 1943.

CHAPTER 6

The Briefing

On 15 May 1943, the pilots and navigators were told the target, but instructed not to tell the other members of the crew. At last they knew it was not the *Tirpitz*, which was the target everyone seemed to think it was. Also on 15 May 1943, the Senior Air Staff Officer, or SASO as he was known, instructed Wing Commander Dunn to read the draft order and from it compile the signal instruction. Many codenames were required and some had been used during training. Such words as 'Dinghy' and 'Danger' were thought, at first, to be unsuitable, but later thought it unwise to alter them at this late stage.

A special code was devised to enable each aircraft to indicate:

1. That the special weapon had been released correctly.
2. Where, in relation to the target, the weapon had fallen.
3. The condition of the target.

On the same day, Wallis flew up to Scampton from the Vickers's airfield at Weybridge in a Wellington aircraft. With him were 'Mutt' Summers and Major Kilner, the managing director at Vickers. On arrival Gibson told them that the job was the next day. It was that evening that Wallis faced the nineteen pilots and navigators, and explained the reason for the mission.

On 16 May 1943, the Chief Staff Officer was told that the operation was 'on' for that night. He then went to Scampton and produced the codes for each crew.

All wireless operators were instructed by Wing Commander Dunn in W/T procedure, with actual specimen messages being transmitted on a buzzer circuit. The use of button 'C' would serve as a reserve frequency by the second group of aircraft. The code word 'Codfish' went by W/T and the signal to bring the reserve frequency into force.

Main Gate, RAF Scampton, 1978. © Alan Cooper

From take-off to zero hour, all aircraft were to maintain a listening watch on the TR 1196 R/T set using button 'D' at 0300E. The VHF set was to be set ten minutes before the target was reached and used until one hour after the completion of the attack, when the operators were to revert to the 1196. All R/T was to be in simple language and conform to the system used during ground practice. In the event of the leader's R/T becoming faulty, he was to inform either aircraft No. 2 or No. 4 to transmit the code word 'Deafness' by W/T twice. They were also briefed to maintain a continuous listening watch on 4090 kcs thoughout the operation, except when passing the 'Operation Completed' signal on 3680 kcs. In the event of a complete failure of control on VHF, the leader of the first wave was to transmit by W/T the code word 'Mermaid', which meant jamming. On all W/T the following code words were to be used:

Prange:	Attack target 'X'
Nigger:	Target 'X' breached, divert to target 'Y'
Dinghy:	Attack target D
Edward:	Attack target E

Fraser: Attack target F
Mason: All aircraft return to base
Apple: First wave listen out on Button B
Codfish: Jamming on button A, change to button C
Mermaid: Jamming on all R/T control by W/T
Tulip: No. 2 take over control at target 'X'
Cracking: No. 4 take over control at target 'Y'
Gilbert: Attack last resort targets as detailed
Goner: Bomb released.

Group HQ would repeat the whole message twice using full power. Should W/T be used, each aircraft was to call the leader of the group by W/T as soon as it arrived over the target. Instruction would then be given by the leader (Gibson) as to what target to attack.

On 16 May 1943, at 1800 hours on a fine sunny day, all 133 men were assembled in the airmen's dining hall. It would be the longest Bomber Command briefing of the war, with forty-one sets of instructions to be read and learned by the crews. On guard outside were three air force policemen. Of the twenty-one crews only nineteen were selected. It was said that there was illness in Flight Lieutenant Wilson's crew,

The briefing room, RAF Scampton, 1978. © *Alan Cooper*

and Sergeant Divall, having arrived much later for training; was not ready for the big day. The exact facts about this are obscure and not clear.

The first person to speak at the briefing was the Air Officer Commanding 5 Group, Ralph Cochrane. He said, 'Bomber Command has been delivering the bludgeon blow on Hitler; you have been selected to give the rapier thrust which will shorten the war. If it is successful.'

It was then Gibson's turn, he pulled back two curtains, behind which were three large photographs of the dams, also a large map showing the routes to them, plus table models of the dams which had been made at RAF Medmenham, the home of Photographic Intelligence. Flying Officer Dave Rodger remembers his pilot, Joe McCarthy saying 'It sure looks big to breach.' Gibson went on to explain the plan, that the squadron would fly from Scampton in three groups, or waves, to attack the Mohne, Eder and Sorpe in moonlight at low-level. The three attack groups would be:

Group 1:   Nine Lancasters in three sections, spaced at ten minute intervals, each consisting of three aircraft led by Gibson. They would take the southern route to the target area and attack 'X' – The Mohne Dam. The attack would last until the dam had clearly been breached. It was estimated it would take three attacks to breach the dam. When this had been achieved the leader would divert those that had not attacked the dam to target 'Y' – The Eder Dam. Here the same tactics as at the Mohne would apply. Should both be breached, any remaining aircraft of the first group that had not released its bomb would fly to the Sorpe – target 'Z'.

Group 2:   Five Lancasters led by Squadron Leader McCarthy and manned by crews who would take the northern route to the target. They would cross the enemy coast at precisely the same time as the leading three Lancasters of the first group, but at a different point. This second group would attack the Sorpe, and flying in from the north would act as a diversionary force for the first group.

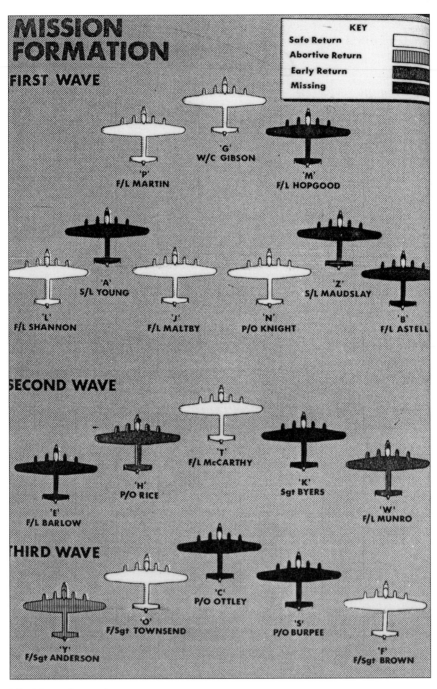

The Dams formation

Group 3 and Final Group: This consisted of the remaining six Lancasters led by Flight Sergeant Bill Townsend, who would form an airborne reserve under the control of Group HQ. They would also fly the southern route to the target, but their take-off time would be such that they could be recalled before crossing the enemy coast if the first and second groups had successfully breached all three targets.

In British airspace the groups would fly at 1,500 feet, but on crossing the English coast they would come down to 60 feet, using the spotlights to determine the height off the sea. Gibson's deputy would be Young and his deputy, if need be, was Maudslay.

For the attack on the Mohne and Eder Dams, each wireless operator would fire a red Very cartridge to let the leader know he was attacking and had released his bomb. Each aircraft was to fly a left handed circuit in the target area to avoid collisions and to give the pilots the clearest view of the target area.

The attack on the Sorpe Dam would be different to the others, with the aim being to drop the bomb near the centre of the dam wall and about 20 feet out, by flying the length of the dam from end to end. The speed was 180 mph slower than the speed for the other dams and as low as possible.

Between each attack, three minutes was to be allowed to let the water subside, assess the damage and see if the dam had been breached or not.

Gibson was followed in the briefing by Wallis, whose opening words were, 'You gentlemen are really carrying out the third of the three experiments. We have tried it out on model dams, also a dam one-fifth of the size of the Mohne Dam. I cannot guarantee it will come off, but I hope it will.' After the briefing he said, 'They must have thought it was Father Christmas talking to them.'

The briefing continued with the AOC of 5 Group, Air Vice-Marshal Ralph Cochrane, who explained the importance of the attack and that it would do tremendous damage to Germany and progress the war. Gibson spoke of the operational details that he had previously given to pilots and navigators. Wing Commander Dunn followed with the signals procedure, the R/T and W/T to be used on the operation and finally at 1930 hours he spoke to the wireless operators. And so the briefing went on with call signs, weather, and the routes. The crews then gathered around the models of the dams which had been built by Ted Greenman. Photographs of the dams were viewed and route maps checked for every detail. The route was 400 miles and much care had gone into avoiding flak positions. Wing Commander Percy Pickard, DSO, DFC, helped a great deal in the planning of a twisting course through the coastal defences, trying not to come any nearer than a mile of any known defences. Flight Lieutenant 'Hoppy' Hopgood noted that one he had seen on a previous operation when flying over the town of Huls, where a large rubber factory was heavily defended, had been missed. He was able to re-route this and miss going over or near the town.

The Met officer predicted good weather over the target and most importantly a full moon, which would rise at 1700 hours on 16 May and set at 0454 hours on the morning of 17 May 1943.

Outside, the trucks were rolling across the airfield, loaded with huge cylindrical bombs covered with tarpaulin, the bombs still warm from the 4 tons of special high explosives put in at Woolwich Arsenal. The ground crew had their work cut out getting nineteen Lancasters ready. This involved fitters, electricians, riggers, armourers, parachute workers, flying controllers, intelligence staff, clerks, police, cooks, mess staff and transport; all who had a special job and were a vital cog in a very large wheel.

The all up weight for each Lancaster on take-off was:

Lancaster and crew:	40,000lbs
Petrol (1740 gallons):	12,550lbs
Oil (150 gallons):	1,350lbs
Bomb:	9,100lbs

The bomb had originally weighed 11,600lbs, but had been reduced by the removal of the wood covering.

A recce on 16 May 1943 had shown the water four feet from the top of the dam. It also showed that the Mohne was the only dam defended with anti-torpedo nets in front of the dam, spread in a double boom. There were also three 3-inch anti-aircraft guns to the north of the dam and possibly three or four light guns in the dam towers.

The ribbing that 617 Squadron had received from 57 Squadron, in appearing to being a non-operational squadron, stopped as soon as they sensed that something big was afoot.

After the briefing Squadron Leader 'Dinghy' Young went over to Wing Commander Wally Dunn and said how nice it was to see him again, having seen him at many briefings on many occasions at Driffield with 103 Squadron.

There was one sad moment before the raid when 'Nigger', Guy Gibson's dog, was killed outside the main gate at Scampton. It was, even in wartime, a very busy road and it was said that the car was a taxi; being dark and 'Nigger' black in colour, the driver may not have even seen him. 'Nigger' had been with Guy for over two years and after drinking numerous pints of beer in the officers' mess the night before, would fly on the exercises with Gibson the next day, he usually curled up in the Perspex dome at the front of the aircraft. Flight Sergeant 'Chiefy' Powell told Aircraftman Crosby, Wing Commander Gibson's batman, not to tell his 'Boss' until after the raid, but he did let it slip out, probably when Gibson asked him where 'Nigger' was. 'Chiefy' went down to the guardroom where 'Nigger's' body had been taken and placed in one of the cells. He had been killed outright. Gibson asked 'Chiefy' to bury the dog outside his office in Hangar No. 2 at midnight, about the time he would be over the Mohne Dam.

For the staff at the officers' mess the telltale signs of an operation were there. Two eggs and bacon for aircrew on operations. They were served by Leading Aircraft Woman Edna Broxholme and fellow waitress Leading Aircraft Woman Norma Hubbard. Morfydd Brooks remembers the crews coming out of the briefing looking grim and strained, the usual banter was missing and despite trying to jolly them up, it did not help. One of those that went to the officers' mess for supper was Barnes Wallis, but he had little appetite to eat, his mind was on the next few hours.

Gibson's flight engineer Sergeant John Pulford's father had died and he was allowed to attend his funeral in Hull. He was escorted by two RAF policemen, known as 'Snowdrops' because of their white caps, and was not allowed to mix with the people at the funeral in case he let anything slip about the operation that night. To some he must have looked like a deserter.

CHAPTER 7

Target One – The Mohne

At about 2030 hours on 16 May 1943 the crews were out at the aircraft. In the case of Dave Shannon he was a little late arriving at the transport from the officer's mess, it was thought at the time that he was saying goodbye to his girlfriend, later his wife Ann, who was a WAAF officer at Scampton.

Apart from Tony Burcher and Jim Fraser, one from Australia and the other Canada, John Hopgood's crew were playing cricket on the grass, Tony and Jim were quite content to sit and have their own thoughts. Both were very experienced, Tony having finished a tour with Gibson's previous squadron (106) and Jim having flown on operations with 50 Squadron. The way things later turned out it was ironic that these two had not joined in the cricket match.

Ken Earnshaw, Hopgood's navigator, said to Jim Fraser before take-off, 'I don't think we are coming home.'

Gibson seemed very relaxed, which one assumes comes with great experience. Having lost Nigger, his soul mate for two years, it seemed he was trying desperately not to think too much, other than on the task ahead.

As Ken Brown sat on the grass, Pilot Officer Burpee, a fellow Canadian, came over and put his hand out saying, 'Goodbye Ken.' Ken had a strong feeling that Burpee would not come back. There were men in Bomber Command who could look at a man and know that this was their last operation, Ken was one of those men.

On boarding the aircraft the bomb aimer would go first, entering the Lancaster by the starboard rear door, up a small rung ladder, then turned right and made his way towards the nose of the aircraft, his home for the whole of the trip. To do this in flying kit and flying boots etc. was not easy with two supports to climb over, the second spar and the main spar, which was about five feet in height (Author – I have done it in ordinary clothes and it's not easy). Once he reached the nose of the aircraft he had to lay prone on a padded rest under his chest. On his left was the bombing panel with many switches and controls. Above him for this operation was the front gunner, sitting astride his two .303 machine guns, with his feet in two special stirrups to keep them out of the way of the bomb aimer. The next man up was the pilot, who made his way in the same way as the bomb aimer and into his left hand padded seat. Here he would sit for the next eight to nine hours. A comfortable seat that, when in it, you seem to be on top of Everest. He was followed by the flight engineer, who would sit on a folding seat opposite the pilot. On take-off he would help the pilot by putting his hand under the pilot's to make sure the throttles did not slip, as this could result in a loss of power, which on take-off was fatal. During the flight his role was to keep an eye on the petrol, oil pressure and an experienced ear listening to the Lancaster's Merlin engines. Many flight engineers had been pre-war car mechanics before joining the RAF. The navigator followed and took the seat behind the pilot at a table about three feet by four. He was followed by the wireless operator, who sat behind the navigator with only the wireless equipment separating them. At his right hand the morse key and on his left a small window where he had an excellent view of the port engines, and if required, could be covered by a blind or curtain. Last but not least the rear gunner, who instead of turning right went left and made his way to his lonely rear turret, he would not see the rest of the crew until they landed back in the UK, on his way he passed the Elsan portable toilet and through two folding doors which were designed to keep out the draught, but more so fire. His position, to say the least, was cramped and as many rear gunners will remember, it was cold. The outside temperature of Europe in wintertime at 40 below, it was the most uncomfortable thing. To make sure they had a clear view, many gunners had the central glass panel removed, the slightest smudge of oil on the glass could – at night – look like a fighter coming into attack.

When the crew were aboard the 'after starting' check began from the pilot to the rest of the crew. External power supply removed and clear; radiator shutters open; booster coil off; vacuum pumps changeover cock, suction reading; flaps operational check, up and off; selector neutral; check all fuel tanks, booster pumps on and off; engine temperatures and pressure within limits. Then the pre-taxi checks, pre-take-off checks and finally clearance to set the brakes and ease the throttles to full boost.

One of the first aircraft due to take-off was Flight Lieutenant Joe McCarthy's, ED923 – 'Q-Queenie'. He had received a red Very light to start up engines and proceed, but on attempting to start up he found one engine had a leak in the engines coolant system. They rushed across the runway heading for ED 825 – 'T-Tommy', the reserve aircraft. On reaching the other aircraft Dave Rodger found the centre panel of his rear turret in place, so with the help of the ground crew they smashed it out so he could have a clear view.

As Joe McCarthy settled in the reserve aircraft 'T-Tommy' he discovered the compass card, which was vital for accurate flying and carefully chartered the route to the dams, was missing. Without it his chances of getting through the enemy defences was nil. As he got out to look for the card, the ripcord on his seat parachute was pulled and his parachute billowed out. All was well however when 'Chiefy' Powell turned up with the missing card and a replacement parachute. Finally, but twenty minutes behind time, he took off, it was 2201 hours. Three aircraft had taken off prior to this, Barlow at 2128 hours, followed by Munro, Byers, and Geoff Rice. Despite being the last off, McCarthy would be the only one to reach the target (Sorpe) and drop his bomb.

The next wave off was Gibson, Hopgood, and Mick Martin, they got off at 2139 hours followed by Young, Maltby, and Shannon at 2147 hours and lastly Maudslay, Astell and Knight at 2159 hours.

Before taking off, Albert Garshowitz, in Barlow's crew, had chalked on the bouncing bomb 'Never has so much been expected of so few', on seeing this, Frank Garbas, from Hamilton, Ontario, laughed with the rest of the crew and climbed aboard. He knew Albert's wit as they were boyhood friends and had played football together at Eastwood Park in Hamilton. In the dining room of his parents' home was a 6 × 10 coloured picture of Frank in his blue RCAF uniform.

Prior to the crew leaving, Sergeant Jim Heveron had the task of collecting wallets and next-of-kin letters, which were kept in the orderly room office safe. All the WAAFs and ground crew who were not on duty came out to see them off.

Ken Brown took off on the grass and not the runway, as is shown in later films etc. The bomb he had below him had 11,960lbs marked on the side. This transpired from when the bomb was made with a casing and wooden cover, it was what it weighed before the casing and cover were removed for the raid. He found that to keep the aircraft in the air he had to use a climbing power of 2650 rpm at 9 (boost). They then went down to 60 feet to try out the guns and the lights. The lights, when focused on the water, formed a figure eight. They also tried out the motor that rotated the bomb, with this going around Ken found flying the Lancaster was like flying a truck over the rails of a railway track with it being so unbalanced.

Corporal Bryden watched the aircraft fly low then format over Scampton. Leading Aircraftman Nick Carr, Leading Aircraftman Keith Stretch and Leading Aircraftman D.F. Payne, who had worked on Gibson's aircraft 'G-George' and also Young's 'J-Johnny', watched them go. Leading Aircraftman Keith Stretch had organized a stand-in for his shift that evening. When the aircraft had left he climbed through a hedge at the back of the airfield and was confronted by his stand-in Ray Fisher, he said, 'They have gone and I think it's the real thing!' The ground crew thoughts were, 'where have they gone and what is the target?'

In the main 617 Squadron were the only aircraft sent out that night. Apart that is from the diversionary operations such as the Mosquitoes of 2 Group who were despatched to Berlin, two on Kiel, two on Cologne and two on Munster. Two Stirlings of 15 Squadron, four from 75 Squadron, two from 49 Squadron and six from 218 Squadron, plus two Lancasters of 115 Squadron laying mines off the Frisian Islands – which in Bomber Command was known as gardening. From 196, 432 and 466 Squadrons, Wellingtons were laying mines off Brest, Lorient and St Nazaire. No. 290 Operational Training Unit, part of 92 Group, had four Wellingtons dropping leaflets over Orleans. Two Halifaxs of 138 Special Duties Squadron were operating with the resistance over France, and 161 Squadron, also a special duties squadron, were operating over Denmark in similar work. It was unusual for Bomber Command to launch large-scale attacks during full moon periods, for obvious reasons the Mosquitoes were used for their nuisance value. The mine-laying operations would help to take the attention off the low flying 617 Lancasters. It was hoped that the enemy defences on the ground would think they were racing over the coast, and observers might think they were lost or a little off course, but also on mine-laying operations.

On the first leg of the route out, drifts were used across the North Sea. Flame floats were used, also GEE, the aircrafts navigational aid, they were used quite a lot over Europe on the outward and return trips. The sea crossing was short and the enemy coast was soon spotted by the pilot and bomb aimer with those immortal words in history 'Enemy Coast Ahead Skip.' It was a simple statement but full of thoughts, feelings and emotions. This was the start of any opposition. It was here that the fuse on the bomb would be armed.

The second group were timed to cross the coast at the same time as the leading group, but at a different point, they were the first to hit trouble. Geoff Rice in the second wave had seen gunfire, he saw a Lancaster hit by ground fire as it went over Vlieland on the Dutch coast at 300 feet and watched it go down at Texel, the time was 2257 hours. This would have been Byers, who it appears was further south than he should have been, owing to the Nocturnal Jet Stream with a 20 to 30 knot north-east wind at surface level and after a warm sun during the day. He had crashed at Waddenzee, a few miles from Texel, he and all his crew killed. His bomb exploded weeks later.

Geoff himself was not immune from trouble as he reached the Zyder Zee, hugging the surface of the water which was dark and unforgiving, he hit the water. He pulled up the stick but the damage was already done. The underside of the Lancaster was torn out and with it the bomb. So much water came in that Sergeant Burns, his rear gunner, was up to his knees in water and at one time the water came over his turret. The tailwheel had been forced up into the aircraft, breaking the main spar of the tailplane and finishing up near the Elsan toilet, which was near the rear door. Further forward, the inspection panels in the floor of the flight deck and above the bomb bay were spouting with water, and soaking the navigator McFarlane's charts.

He had no option without a weapon but to return to base. But even this was not an easy task, not having a tailwheel he landed on his main wheels and held the tail up until the last moment, when he finally let it down the tail fins hit the runway with a huge crash. He got out and sat on the grass wondering what to do next, all that training and nothing to show for it. He felt he had let 617 down. The station commander, Group Captain Charles Whitworth, turned up in his car and took Geoff and the rest of the crew back to the ops room where Harris was waiting for them. Geoff was expecting to be taken to the cleaners, but not a bit of it, Harris was very sympathetic and said how lucky they were. His reaction and understanding stayed with Geoff all his life.

Gibson and the leading section had also reached the coast. The plan had been to fly between two Dutch islands at Haltern, off the coast of Holland, although both were known to have heavy anti-aircraft defences. He came under fire at 0011 hours from light flak and all three in the group were picked up by searchlights. Gibson turned his aircraft into a severe turn and out of the beam before continuing on route. Hopgood was one of the three caught in the searchlights and also took evasive action. Tony Burcher was in his rear turret thinking of his bride to be, Joan, a WAAF whom he was due to marry on 12 June when he heard Pilot Officer George Gregory, DFM, a Glaswegian, shout, 'Bloody Hell!' from the front turret and he thought they were going to hit the ground, but Hopgood got the aircraft under control and was able to gain height. For a second Tony saw the looping arc of a high tension cable above his line of vision, when he looked back he saw the cable drop away behind the aircraft, they had in fact gone under the cable. Hopgood apologized to the rest of the crew.

Wallis at this time was waiting at HQ 5 Group. He had asked Gibson if he could fly with him, but of course being a civilian, he was turned down.

Back at Scampton, George Powell and Corporal John Bryden had the sad task of burying, as requested by Gibson, his dog 'Nigger.' They buried the dog in front of No. 2 Hangar and in view of Gibson's office; it was marked with a simple wooden cross made by one of the 'chippies' (woodworker) on the station. (Today it is still there, the simple wooden cross has been replaced with a beautiful inscribed stone and surrounded by a rail enclosure.) 'Chiefy' Powell made a point of visiting the grave on many occasions after the war.

While the leading group were nearing the Mohne, Les Munro and Robert Barlow were still on route to the Sorpe; McCarthy was behind, desperately trying to make up time. The overland route to the target consisted of short dog-legs of perhaps fifteen miles, planned to avoid flak positions. GEE was working well.

Munro had flown to the southern end of the island of Vlieland where he changed course to the south-east, across the Zyder Zee. But as soon as they did so a flak ship, whose positions are difficult to calculate, opened up on them as they flew over and were silhouetted in the night sky. A hole was torn amidships, the intercom was put out

Guy Gibson with 'Nigger', 1942

of action and the W/T rendered useless. He continued on for some time, thinking all the time of what to do next. He decided to ask the crew what they thought of the situation, his flight engineer Frank Appleby, passed a note around saying, 'Intercom useless, should we go on after all the training and hard work?' Jim Clay, the bomb aimer, replied, 'We will be a menace to the rest of the force with no intercom and no way of communicating with the rest of the aircraft.' He had a point as communications were vital on such an operation as this, as was the consideration of the rest of the crew and their safety. Bill Howarth from Oldham, in the front turret, felt the aircraft turn to the left and he asked Jim if they were returning to base. Jim just nodded –

'Nigger's' well-
kept grave at
RAF Scampton.
© Alan Cooper

they were heading back desperately disappointed, but in the circumstances they had no other choice.

On reaching Scampton they were met by 'Chiefy' Powell and Jim
Heveron. They both saw what they thought was the bomb, but without its arm clamps on each side and made a hasty retreat. 'Capable'
Caple, the armaments officer, rode up on his bike and told them it
was only the fuel pipes hanging down and not the bomb arms. On the
return journey Les Munro had jettisoned fuel to lessen the load. They
landed at 0036 hours.

Tony Burcher had, in his pocket, a stone which he carried for good
luck. It had been given to him by a boy in January whose parents had

been killed in an air raid. He asked Tony the next time he was over
Germany would he drop the stone on the Germans for him. Tony
had never thrown it out, but kept it as a lucky charm and so far it had
worked.

Hopgood asked Tony to keep his eyes peeled. His four .303 guns
were loaded with tracer, as were all the guns for this operation,
instead of the usual one trace shell to five bullets, when they tried
them out in the gun butts at Scampton Tony had more stoppages than
usual. He had opened up on the searchlights when they were coned,
when suddenly the Lancaster was raked from nose-to-tail from the
ground. He was hit in the stomach and groin by shell splinters, again
a searchlight blazed in his face, he returned this with a long burst
upon which the light went out. Then came a shell burst alongside his
turret. He heard the flight engineer say, 'The port engine's gone Skip,
oil is coming out and burning like hell!'

'I'm feathering,' came the reply from Hopgood. He himself had
been hit in the face and was bleeding. When Tony tried to rotate his
turret he found it was not working, all power from the port engine,
which controlled the hydraulics, had failed. What he thought was
saliva in his mouth was blood. He then heard Sergeant John Minchin
the wireless operator say, 'I have been hit and cannot move my leg
Skip. Skip,' Tony then reported to Hopgood that he also had been
hit. From the front turret gunner, Gregory, there was no reply, it was
assumed he had been killed or seriously wounded and unable to
respond. Hopgood was also wounded, he had a serious head wound
with blood pouring out of it. Despite this he said, 'carry on and don't
worry.' He asked the flight engineer to hold a handkerchief to his
head. All this conversation Tony could hear on the intercom.

A message was sent to Gibson by VHF telling him that they had
been hit, but were carrying on. Flight Lieutenant Mick Martin was
okay and on track to the Mohne Dam. Alongside him Hopgood
was somehow able to fly on to the target.

At 0011 hours Gibson reported back that he had come under fire
again. A moment later another Lancaster came under fire. Bill Astell
flew down a canal to search for a pinpoint when Flying Officer Knight
and his navigator 'Hobby' Hobday saw Astell's aircraft come under
fire; there was an explosion and seven men died. It would appear
Astell, in an attempt to avoid the ground fire, hit a high voltage cable,
breaking the point of the pylon which was 30 metres high. The area
was Estate Achling Aabeck, ten kilometres over the Dutch/German

border, and north of Dorsten, the time 0015 hours. The gunfire had come from the air base at Dorsten, but for some reason the crash report was not sent to the police until 0359 hours.

As Gibson flew over the North Sea, Taerum, his navigator, found that they were off the planned route, so Gibson pulled up to 300 feet to get landmarks. Taerum saw a windmill etc. and realized they had drifted off to starboard, so he gave Gibson a new course. From there on, part of the route was worked by Spafford who used a special roller to identify important features such as railway lines and canals and to avoid high tension wires, but again they lost their way, owing to strong wings having pushed them further south. Mick Martin learned of this from his rear gunner Tammy Simpson, when his aircraft arrived over the Mohne first, followed by Hopgood and Gibson.

Guy Gibson reached the Mohne Dam at 0015 hours and gave instructions for the force under his command to stand-by, John Pulford pressed the switch to start the bomb revolving. This was about seven minutes before making an attack. Gibson then radioed, 'Hello all Cooler aircraft I am going in to attack.' Terry Taerum was responsible for the height, as they approached the target he switched on the two spotlights. It was 0025 hours as they made the approach. Looking down he could clearly see they were on, but were still some distance apart. Spam Spafford, in the nose, activated the self-destructing bomb fuse as they made the run-in, Pulford monitored the speed at about 232 mph. Spafford began to line up his special bombsight on to the dam's twin towers.

Colonel Karl Burke, commander of the SS Flak Unit was based on the dam. One of his men was Karl Schutte, on duty in the north tower and he remembered it being very quiet. Apart from the sentry walking up and down it was silent. Then out of the silence the telephone rang, it was warning of an air attack. The gun crews were put on warning and they waited and then came the sound of engines from low flying aircraft. The guns on the tower opened fire, to which the aircraft returned the fire. Then came flares from the aircraft and the gunners on the tower were blinded. The first bomb from Gibson was dropped, falling short of the wall, but followed by a huge spout of water up to 100 feet high, which came over the dam wall.

George Deering in the front turret opened fire on the towers; the bomb had been dropped at 0028 hours rotating at 500 rpm, speed 230 mph. It bounced three times and was seen to slam into the parapet and dead on target between the towers. Hutchison fired a red Very flare over the dam as a signal to the others that they had made their attack. In the rear turret Trevor-Roper returned the fire coming from the towers on the dam.

As Gibson made his attack, another aircraft flown by Flight Lieutenant Robert (Bob) Barlow, had flown into a high voltage cable and crashed south-east of Emmerich at a place called Hedden in Rees-on-Rhine, all the crew were killed.

At 5 Group HQ, Harris, Cochrane and Wallis waited for news; the first signal that Wally Dunn picked up was the flak warning from Gibson. And then that he had dropped his bomb, but no breach. 'Goner – 68A time 0037.' This translated as bomb released and exploded five yards from the dam, no apparent breach. On a blackboard was the list of the aircraft taking part in the attack. On a dais alongside the opposite wall sat the operations officer Wally Dunn, he was in telephone contact with the radio room.

As well as the gunners on the dam, the foreman of the power station which was below the dam, Herr Clemen Kohler, heard from a look-out at 0020 hours of the possible arrival of enemy aircraft. He then realized it was a full moon night, a night when normally the RAF did not operate or venture over the Reich, also that the water level in the lake was higher than it had ever been before. He telephoned the United Electricity Company of Westphalia's Officer at Neheim, a little town just down the valley. He told them he thought the RAF were attacking the dam, but, perhaps understandably, he was not believed, so he put down the phone, opened the door and looked out. It was then that Gibson's Lancaster flew overhead with all guns firing, then came the explosion from his bomb and water began spilling over the dam wall high above him. Kohler began to run and did not stop until he reached the side of the valley several hundred yards away. He dropped down beneath a tree halfway up the slope, where he looked back down to see if the dam was still intact, to his surprise and relief it was.

Gibson waited a few minutes for the water disturbance to subside, when it had, he called in the next aircraft – John Hopgood, who had already been hit and damaged. The value of Gibson's first run was he was able to gauge the barometer pressure over the water at the prescribed height. He was also able to judge the firepower from the dams, which seemed to be about fifteen guns, not only on the towers but on the banks each side of the dam. Gibson called in Hopgood and said, 'Take over 'M-Mother'. Good luck.' In the rear turret of 'M-Mother' the wounded Tony Burcher had seen Gibson's attack while they circled around to see if they were needed or not.

As they went in Hopgood said on the intercom, 'Stand by, rear gunner, they are putting up a barrage ahead.' As they went in Gibson was trying to draw some of the fire off them, he saw Hopgood's spotlights go on over the water, upon which they attracted all the fire-power from the dams; Gibson was determined to fight their corner.

Karl Schutte, manning the guns on the dam related his memories: 'Target change, new in-flight. It roared towards us like a beast as if it would ram the tower and us. One did not think of the danger, at last we could fire. I stood behind the gunner adjusting the gun heights and making corrections, at the same time adjusting the side directions. We fired whatever the gun would give. The shells whipped into the face of the attacker.'

Tony Burcher heard a shout from the navigator Ken Earnshaw to, 'Go lower, still lower!' as he watched the two spotlights join up.

He then heard, 'Bomb gone!' from Jim Fraser the bomb aimer.

At that moment came a terrific crash and Tony saw flames scream-ing past his turret on the port side. Then came a shout from Sergeant Brennan, the flight engineer, 'we're on fire, port inner engine.'

Hopgood said, 'Press the extinguisher and feather Number Two engine.' For a few seconds this worked but then the fire relit itself. The port outer engine was dead and the port inner engine blazing. His options were few at this low height so he instantly gave the order that no member of a crew wants to hear, 'Abandon aircraft.'

His bomb was now bouncing its way to the dam wall, but having been released a second or so late, bounced over the wall and exploded, destroying the power station below the wall.

Tony Burcher tried to crank his turret round by means of the dead man's handle and remembered doing it in record time. This was so he could get to his parachute which was stored inside the fuselage, but until he got the turret in the correct position and in line with the exit doors he could not get out to get it. When it was, he pressed the door release, got out and grabbed his chute and clipped it to his chest. Once this was done he plugged into his intercom and said, 'How are you doing up front?'

Upon which Hopgood shouted back to him, 'Get out you bloody fool. If only I had another 300 feet – I can't get any more height.'

All this took place in no more than twenty-five seconds after passing over the dam wall. On fire in the starboard wing and with a flame like a giant torch, Hopgood flew over the town of Haar, disappeared and was heard to crash.

The flak gunners on the wall had seen the hits on 'M-Mother' and shouted, 'It's on fire', a giant mushroom of foam came up in front of the wall, then the detonation reached them, the pressure was so great those watching were flung off their feet. Karl Schutte remembers the firing being good but he did not have too much time to dwell on their success as a hot gun barrel needed to be changed and oiled. A report came from Tower Two; 'Out of Action' the impact had thrown it into the plinth.

Jim Fraser pulled his ripcord in the aircraft, went out of the escape hatch and then pulled the chute out behind him, as he did the tail-wheel of the Lancaster went over his head. He swung vertically and within three seconds he had touched the ground, if he had gone out and then pulled his chute he would have been on the ground before it opened and not survived. The Lancaster crashed about 1,500 to 2,000 feet away from him. He had come down three miles to the north-west, near Ostonnen, five miles from Soest.

As Hopgood tried to keep control in order to get his crew out, Tony Burcher saw the wireless operator John Minchin, who had been badly wounded over the coast; he was dragging himself along the length of the fuselage towards the rear. His face was white with pain; his leg had nearly been severed. Tony did all he could to help him and clipped on his chute and pushed him out into the darkness. As he did so he pulled Minchin's D-rain release on his parachute, he did not see it open, but it was seen that two chutes opened up so maybe he did land safely, but he died of his injuries. Tony had already realized, as did Jim Fraser, the only chance he had was to open the chute in the aircraft, which he did and bundling it up under his arm he plugged in his intercom once more and said, ' Rear gunner abandoning aircraft.'

The reply from Hopgood was, 'For Christ's sake get out of here!'

At that moment there was a terrific bang and rush of air and Tony was blown out, the flames had reached the wing fuel tank and exploded, as he came out he hit the tailplane so hard that it was later found he had broken his back. To the day he died Tony had a hollow in his back and the break could be felt and seen in an X-ray. He landed with a thud; at the height he came out, it's no wonder the landing was a hard one. As he hit the ground his chute took him back up, this, the German Medical Officer said later, is what saved him. For a while he lay there stunned, he heard the aircraft overhead and the ground vibrating under him. Dan Walker, Dave Shannon's navigator, had seen 'Hoppy' go down and was amazed after the war to learn that Tony Burcher had survived. The Lancaster, he remembered, was speeding itself along the ground in flames.

Jim Fraser landed in a wheat field, hid his chute in a culvert and when dawn came watched from his hiding place as hundreds of Germans came out to see what had happened to the dam. He was able to get through the cordon of enemy soldiers and headed towards Holland. After ten days on the run he was captured, only thirty miles from the border. The next weeks were in Dulag Luft, an interrogation camp for downed aircrew and run by the Luftwaffe. For the next two years he was in four different camps, one being Stalag Luft III, the camp from which the great escape was activated in March 1944. His wife got a letter from him dated 19 June 1943 saying he was safe and a prisoner of war.

It was then Mick Martin's turn and Gibson called him in. He flew alongside to take some of the fire from the dam's guns. Despite this Martin was hit a number of times, his starboard outer fuel tank and ailerons were damaged, luckily the tank was empty at the time. Tony Foxlee, in the front guns, was returning the fire and Tammy Simpson in the rear turret followed this up as they passed over the dam. Martin's bomb went down at 0038 hours, at the time there was still a lot of smoke from the burning remains of the power house. The bomb bounced and could not be seen because of this, but then came a huge water spout and ripples spreading out, followed by a huge wave spilling over the dam wall. His bomb had veered off, maybe because the bomb had been dropped on the tarmac when loading up at Scampton.

Karl Schutte had now only two guns in action, the others having been knocked out by the aircraft gunners. Again, he said, engines came nearer with banking planes dropping flares.

They started to fire at the spotlights underneath the approaching aircraft. They had to admit that with only 2cm guns left in action, any hits they recorded on the aircraft would be sheer luck. The aircraft continued to fire at them, Karl described it as like a string of pearls; the luminous spur of the shells came towards the towers like large glow-worms. Then, he went on to say, came an explosion and a great waterspout, the lake quaked and mighty waves engulfed the wall.

They did not know if the dam was intact or not, but did know they must keep firing again and again. Then came the fourth attack and the picture was repeated. Karl hoped that no other guns would be out of action. Since the three guns of the 2nd Unit were down in Gunne, they could only fire on the aircraft – or machines as he called them – that were coming from the lakeside and were veering away.

The next to attack was 'Dinghy' Young, he dropped his bomb at 0040 hours and again his gunners took on the men on the dam. The bomb bounced up to the dam wall and again a waterspout with the water spilling over the dam wall. Young called Gibson and said he thought the dam had gone, but when Gibson looked down as he circled around he found it was still intact, one more bomb and it would go. Young sent a message back to 5 Group at 0050 hours, 'Code 78A – weapon released and exploded in contact with the dam wall, no breach seen.' Mick Martin, who had bombed the dam before Young, for some reason did not send his message until 0053 hours, 'Code 58A – spun weapon, released, exploded yards from dam, no apparent breach.' The next in was 'J-Johnny' and Dave Maltby.

Now there was no firepower coming from the dam wall. As Karl related, machines were firing at them from the valley end, but as they replied the guns failed – the lock was stuck. They tried to unblock the problem, but a premature shell had damaged the housing of the gun, so it was impossible and they were now defenceless. He said at the time, 'We waited literally for the end.'

As Maltby came in the only gun still firing, but not from the dam wall, was on the lower wall, Karl could see the pilot as the aircraft came in and all they could do was watch it. They resorted to a drill, when their guns were out of action, of using rifles. Again Maltby was on target and the water flew into the air. When it cleared, a hole could be seen in the dam and it was getting bigger by the moment. It transpired that although Maltby helped, it was Young's bomb that had created the breach, a minor breach was seen as Maltby dropped his bomb. Maltby's wireless operator Anthony Stone sent a message back to base at 0055 hours, 'Code 78A – weapon released exploded in contact with the wall no breach apparent.'

Back at base they were getting disturbed; five hits but no breach. But all was well when Gibson sent a message back at 0056 hours with the pre-arranged code word 'Nigger'. As Wally Dunn began to take it down, he got to 'N-I-G' and shouted out loud at the top of his voice,

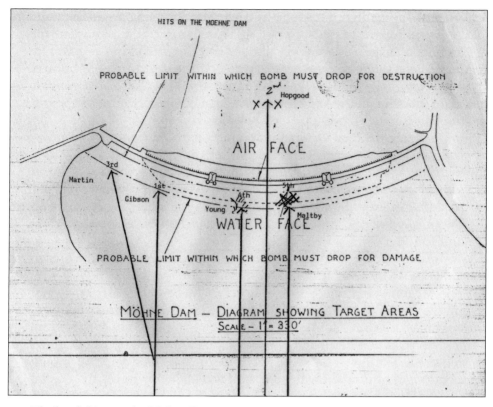

HITS ON THE MOEHNE DAM

PROBABLE LIMIT WITHIN WHICH BOMB MUST DROP FOR DESTRUCTION

2nd Hopgood

AIR FACE

Martin 3rd

Gibson 1st 5th

Young 4th Maltby

WATER FACE

PROBABLE LIMIT WITHIN WHICH BOMB MUST DROP FOR DAMAGE

MÖHNE DAM – DIAGRAM SHOWING TARGET AREAS
SCALE – 1" = 330'

The bomb hits on the Mohne Dam

'Nigger', upon which Harris grabbed Wallis's hand and patted him on the back with his congratulations. At 0057 hours 5 Group replied to Gibson and asked him to repeat his signal, to which Gibson replied with one word only – 'Correct.' He had been about to call in Shannon to attack the dam when through the smoke he saw the dam had rolled over, and ordered him to break off the attack, when he looked again he saw a breach of 150 yards in the dam wall.

Karl watched with horror as the water rushed down the valley, the air full of spray.

Lieutenant Freswinkle, who had also been on the dam, had given orders to his gunners to fire sustained automatic fire through all the apertures in the tower and wall, but it was all a token gesture.

Gibson spent another three minutes over the dam then sent Maltby and Martin back to base, where they landed at 0311 and 0319 hours respectively.

Tony Burcher, with his injured back, was still lying on the ground. When he looked towards the dam he saw a huge column of water. He described it like a giant soda siphon, and then a roaring sound. His immediate thought was that he was going to be drowned, he was however, over a mile away, but in his shocked and stunned condition that's what he thought at the time. He managed to drag himself across the field he had landed in and into a culvert to hide.

On the dam the power station foreman, Clemen Kohler, was sitting beneath a tree and watched as the masonry bulged, then burst between the two twin towers. The remains of the power station vanished in seconds in the onrushing water, which was moving at twenty-feet per second, car searchlights changed colour as the water overtook them. There was now no doubt the Mohne Dam had been smashed once and for all.

Back at 5 Group HQ, Harris was keen to get the news of the breach to the USA and President Roosevelt. He went into the silent glass telephone cabinet which was in the corner of the operations room, picked up the 'secret' telephone and asked the WAAF telephone operator to get him the White House in Washington. She turned to Wally Dunn and he reassured her that it was the White House in the USA that was required. The line was soon put through via the American HQ in London, after a little flirting with the WAAF telephonist the United States soldier on the other end put the call through to Sir Charles Portal, the Chief of the Air Staff, who was in Washington with Churchill.

In a place called Neheim, just down the valley from the dam, the first air-raid warning came at 0030 hours. The duty officer at the police station; Lieutenant Dicke, had heard the sound of aero engines, and went to the watchtower in the town hall to assist in assessing the situation. At 0015 hours he had first observed a bright light, and then a muffled explosion. Ten minutes later the telephone rang at the station. It was the police station at Arnsberg enquiring about the bombs. Dicke replied that the bombs had not fallen in the town area, but in the direct area of the dam. Sometime later the architect at Neheim telephoned to say there was a rumour that the dam had been hit, resulting in flooding. The observer station at the dam should have telephoned by now, but no call had been received.

Then came a call from the 'Special Service' to Dicke, this confirmed the worst news: the dam had been hit and water was pouring down the valley. This report was logged at 0050 hours. Dicke then telephoned the Mayor of Neheim informing him of the bad news. He said he would come straight away and to have one of Dicke's men to meet him. A reserve constable was sent, but when he arrived at the Mayor's house, water was already surrounding it. Dicke then sent officers to the most vulnerable parts of the town to alert the 23,000 people in the town. The water then got into the cellar of the post office and destroyed the telephone system some time before 0100 hours. Then came the flood, waves of 39 feet and at 13 mph.

During the 1950s Tony Burcher met a German engineer who told him that 'some darn fool had blown up the power house which caused great problems for years to come.' It was in 1953 that it was rebuilt, ten years after it had been destroyed. Its replacement was put on the side of the dams as opposed to below it.

Tony told this story to Barnes Wallis when he met him at the film premier of *The Dambusters*.

CHAPTER 8

Target Nos 2 and 3 –
The Eder and The Sorpe

Gibson and the members of the first group who had not dropped their bombs had now arrived at the Eder Dam, with them was 'Dinghy' Young, Gibson's deputy leader. Although there were no defences at this dam, finding it was difficult. It had taken only ten minutes flying time from the Mohne Dam. Gibson flew around low trying to pick it out and it was not until his final run that he saw the reservoir, and then the dam itself. He radioed Flight Lieutenant Dave Shannon to make his run, but Shannon was not sure where the dam was either. It was then that Gibson told Hutchison his wireless operator to fire a red flare, upon seeing it Shannon radioed to say he was on his way. The Eder was in a deep valley amongst tree covered hills. At the upper end of the lake, high on a hill of about 1,000 feet stands the castle of Waldeck – or Schloss as it is known – and the home of Count Waldeck (today it is a restaurant and hotel).

At 0132 hours a telephone rang in the local air raid defence control office, Lieutenant Saahr of the SS answered. He was told, 'This is the Warnzentalle, there are British aircraft circling over the Eder Dam.'

In the case of the Mohne Dam, when Clemen Kohler made his call on similar lines, he was not believed, but on this occasion Saahr did believe the call and rang the nearest SS unit, the Third Company of the 603rd Regional Defence Battalion, at Hemforth. The duty officer, a colonel, confirmed there were three aircraft circling the dam and Saahr said he would call him back, but in the meantime he said, 'if an attack begins sound the alarm'. Saahr then telephoned SS Colonel Burke – not the same Burke as on the Mohne Dam – who was commanding officer of the Flak Training Regiment stationed nearby, warning him that flooding was probable within minutes. Burke put lorries with hundreds of men on standby.

Saahr again telephoned to say that the planes were dropping flares and had turned on their searchlights.

Dave Shannon made his first run at 0139 hours, the route to the dam was over the hill with the castle on top and diving steeply to the required height of 60 feet over the water of the reservoir. But it was not satisfactory and the bomb aimer, 32-year-old Sergeant Len Sumpter, who had been in the Grenadier Guards before transferring to the RAF, said to go around again. As Shannon circled back to make another run Gibson called in Henry Maudslay to make a run and Shannon turned away. Maudslay dropped his bomb, which appeared to be dropped late, there were reports that he had been damaged on route and something was hanging below his aircraft which could have affected the dropping of the bomb; it hit the top of the parapet and exploded. As the Lancaster went over the dam Maudslay sent a weak message back on the R/T. The aircraft had been badly damaged and Maudslay was struggling to keep it in the air as it went towards Emmerich. Despite this, his wireless-operator did send a radio message at 0157 hours, 'Goner, 28B, special weapon released, overshot dam, no apparent breach.' The light anti-aircraft post at Emmerich had strict orders not to fire on hostile aircraft and give away the town's location, but when it was seen to be British, flying low and on fire, one gun opened fire, upon which the other joined in. The aircraft was hit and went down, crashing three to five kilometres south-east of Emmerich at a place called Netterden, all the crew were killed.

At 0151 hours, Gibson took time to radio Astell, but not getting any response he tried again at 0153 hours, again it failed. Astell had crashed and all the crew killed an hour and half previously.

Dave Shannon came in for his third run, this time Len Sumpter was happy and dropped his bomb. It bounced twice and sank at the dam wall, again, as at the Mohne, a huge spout of water 1,000 feet high came minutes later. A gap of nine feet was seen towards the east side of the dam. Flying Officer Brian Goodale, DFC, signalled back, 'Goner 79B, special weapon dropped, small breach in dam.' This was timed at 0206 hours. The blast from this bomb is recorded to have short-circuited the 60,000 volt power lines leading across the valley from the generator house.

It was now Les Knight's turn to attack the Eder Dam. He attacked the dam at 0152 hours with the moon on his starboard beam. They flew a dummy run to make sure of clearing both the steep hill and the trees on the top. He then came in and released his bomb, then had to hop over another very steep hill during the run, flying very near the trees on the top. Gibson in the meantime flew alongside him and saw the bomb bounce three times, hit the dam wall, and explode. A message was sent by wireless operator Bob Kellow at 0200 hours, 'Goner 71B, large breach in dam.' He then made a circuit from a few hundred feet and was able to see the start of the flood in the bright moonlight. A spout of water 800 feet high came up from the dam. This time it was a breach of thirty feet below the top, which caused a tidal wave about thirty feet high and was seen half a mile down the valley from the dam. The water was smashing buildings and bridges, while further down cars were overtaken and lost to sight. The front of the flood was like a face of a cliff moving along and was practically perpendicular.

Gibson had signalled back the call-sign 'Dinghy' at 0154 hours, which meant the Eder had been breached. At 0155 hours it was retransmitted by 5 Group at full power for the benefit of the other aircraft.

The workmen on the dam, standing on the generator steps below the dam, felt a dull shock and the building shake. They ran to the main room but the lighting had failed. Masonry came through the roof and in came the water, but they managed to reach the stone steps leading to the bank before the dam wall broke.

Five minutes later the Eder broke. The telephone in Colonel Burke's office rang; it was Leutnant Saahr, 'Herr Colonel,' he said, 'Arolson Post Office has phoned through a report from the 603rd Battalion that the dam had been destroyed. I have tried twice to contact them but all the lines are dead.'

A motorcyclist rode through the main street of Affolden shouting at the top of his voice to the people taking cover following the air raid warning. 'The dam has been hit, the water is coming, everybody out of the cellars, quickly.' The villagers came out of the shelters and cellars, which, in the circumstances was the worst place to be and headed for high ground. As they did, Affolden vanished in a flood of water, while the streets at Hemelfort collapsed.

At 0210 hours, 5 Group HQ signalled to Gibson asking how many aircraft of the first wave were available for 'C' – (Sorpe). Gibson replied at 0211 hours – 'None'. The force under Gibson set off back to base, because of events they would have to be alert for fighters and defences.

Shannon flew back via the Mohne and saw the valley filling up with water; he then hedge hopped back home, when fifty miles from the Mohne his air gunners shot up a train which was stationary. He arrived back at Scampton at 0406 hours. Gibson arrived back at 0415 hours and Les Knight at 0420 hours.

Back at Scampton the reserve force had taken off as planned. Pilot Officer Warner Ottley in 'C-Charlie' took off at 0009 hours, Pilot Officer Lewis Burpee in 'S-Sugar' at 0011 hours, Flight Sergeant Ken Brown in 'F-Freddie' at 0012 hours, Flight Sergeant Bill Townsend in 'O-Orange' at 0014 hours and Flight Sergeant Cyril Anderson in 'Y-York' at 0015 hours. Ken Brown reached the enemy coast at 0130 hours and Townsend a minute later. At 0145 hours 5 Group transmitted a signal to this group of flak ahead.

Flight Lieutenant Joe McCarthy reached the Sorpe Dam and made a run in at 0046 hours at a speed of 180 mph, slower than the Mohne Dam attack of 230 mph, but it was not until after his tenth run did George Johnson the bomb aimer drop his bomb. He was determined to drop his bomb in the right place and a spout of water 1,000 feet high rose into the air. The damage caused crumbling of about 15 to 20 feet along the dam wall. This later necessitated in the Sorpe Dam being drained to half its capacity.

For some unknown reason it was 0300 hours and only twenty-three minutes from Scampton, before Sergeant Len Eaton radioed back with, '79C – Goner, Special Weapon released, exploded in contact with the dam – small breach in dam.' His route out to the dam was uneventful, but because of a faulty compass he was not able to return by the planned route and chose the same route back, the pinpoint of the Zyder Zee being easier to recognize, he landed at 0323 hours. On his return it was found that he had a bullet hole in his starboard tyre, but did not known how it got there as there were no defences at the Sorpe Dam. After going around so many times, Dave Rodger in the rear turret said, 'Get that bomb out of here,' and when it was finally dropped said, 'Thank Christ.' Joe landed with one flat tyre, but managed to hold up the wheel until the aircraft stopped, because of his skill they only spun around once.

No Aldis lamps or spinning of the bomb were required in attacking the Sorpe Dam. The attack on the Sorpe was completely different to the Mohne or Eder Dams. It had no vertical wall and so had to be attacked across the dam which meant coming over the top of a hill and down a slope to the dam, flaps were used to keep to the correct speed and then once the bomb had been dropped, climbing out quickly to avoid the hills ahead. The bomb was dropped from a height of 30 feet; half that at the other two dams. As Gibson was making the second call to Astell, Burpee, on his way to the Sorpe was shot down near Gilkze-Reijen, a Luftwaffe base between Breda and Tilburg in Holland. He was previously seen by Ken Brown off course, being too far north by a mile or so. The plan was to fly around the base, but while flying low he was caught by searchlights only twenty-five metres from the ground, dazzled by the lights and under fire from light flak he dropped even lower in an attempt to get away from the lights and gunfire, but in so doing hit trees and crashed onto the airbase, hitting an MT section housing trucks belonging to the fire and flak personnel. Moments later it exploded and windows and doors on the base were blown in from the blast, which was so great that the HQ building of the resident NJG/2 nightfighters, some 600 to 700 metres away, was completely blown over. The crashed aircraft burned for some time, with columns of smoke and flames reaching high into the air. Exploding ammunition aided the situation. All the main buildings on the base were damaged. A JU88 pilot named Scholl, stationed at the base, witnessed the whole crash and the aftermath. Although Burpee had not reached his target he certainly had kept any opposition from the fighters at this base out of action for some time.

Gibson had signalled to the third wave at 0221 hours. Bill Townsend replied a minute later and received another message, 'Gilbert – attack the target as detailed.' Townsend replied back at 0226 hours, 'Message received.' At 0227 hours Flight Sergeant Anderson received a message from 5 Group, 'Dinghy – target breached, divert to target Z.' (Sorpe)

Pilot Officer Ottley's route to the Lister dam was the same both out and back. At 0230 hours he received a message from 5 Group to say, 'Gilbert' – the signal to divert to the Lister. But nothing further was heard from him. On route near Heesen, north of Hamm, and it would appear, a little off course, he was shot at by 20mm light anti-aircraft fire. The starboard inner engine was hit and burst into flames and the hydraulic system was knocked out. Fred Tees had changed places with Harry Strange, Fred going into the rear turret and Harry into the front turret. The aircraft went into a dive and crashed. The rear end of the aircraft broke away and Fred Tees was thrown clear, he was alive but badly burned. He was taken to a hospital known as 9c and then later to PoW camp No. L6 at Heydekruge. Ottley had been seen by Ken Brown – at 0235 hours – to crash and blow up with a huge explosion.

Flight Sergeant Ken Brown received a call from 5 Group telling him to attack the Sorpe Dam. His journey was eventful; nearly hitting the spires of a church. He also went past the Mohne Dam and saw two large holes and what seemed to be a smaller one between the two towers. He also attacked three troop trains and opened fire on them, killing nine Germans and wounding four others. The fuselage had been hit by flak but nothing vital was damaged. It would appear that Ken had given permission for the air gunners to carry out target practise.

Although Ken signalled back no breach seen, it would appear that further damage had been done to the dam wall with a crumbling of about 300 feet, which enlarged the area of damage made by McCarthy two hours before.

The whole area of the Sorpe was shrouded in mist. Brown had been told there was a church on top of the village; all they saw was the tops of the spires. He tried to align himself on the spires and then got behind the dam on the first run across, as in McCarthy's run. He made eight runs on the dam, but still it was not right to drop the bomb, so he dropped incendiaries on the banks of the lake, this set some of the trees on fire on both sides of the dam. It was not until the tenth run that he dropped his bomb from 500 yards. It was 0314 hours. He signalled back at 0323 hours, 'Goner 78C, special weapon released, exploded on contact with the dam, no apparent breach.' A water-spout of about 1,000 feet came up and with it the Lancaster, which also went up about 800 feet.

On crossing the Zyder Zee on the return journey over the Den Helder peninsular, Brown was coned by a searchlight and fired upon; a shell hit the side of the aircraft creating a large hole but no injury to the crew.

As with Shannon, Brown took the route home past the Mohne Dam, where they found the gunners to be on the alert and active, he felt he had to come back and pay Hopgood a visit. As they came over, from the dam came 20mm and 37mm gunfire, to which his rear gunner Jack Buckley returned fire.

They reached the coast as daylight was starting to come up, searchlights caught them, cannon shells went through the canopy and the side of the aircraft was blown out. He had to go lower to get out of it so he went down a further ten feet. The front gunner took on the guns which were on the sea wall and Brown saw them either falling hit, or diving for cover. He called on the intercom to see if anyone was hit, somehow no one was, but there were holes in the aircraft. They arrived back at Scampton and Brown said, 'This is F-Freddie'.

A voice came back, 'Hello F-for Fox'. Somehow their callsign had changed in the time they had been away. They landed back at Scampton at 0533 hours. After landing they wondered where the rest of the aircraft were, the ground crew were running around with tears running down their faces – so many had no aircraft to tend to. His aircraft was so badly damaged it had to go back to the factory.

Flight Sergeant Cyril Anderson, the other man sent to the Sorpe, was unable to find the lake near Dulmen, as with Brown, he also found it shrouded in mist, when they did reach Dulmen they were coned by searchlights but unable to fire upon them because of a stoppage in the rear turret, he was not able to turn the rear turret fully around. He turned back at 0310 hours, this was a crew decision, as with the dawn coming up he would not reach the target on time. At 0423 hours he reported, 'Returning to base-unsuccessful.' This was unfortunate, as Ken Brown thought that one more bomb would have breached the Sorpe Dam, the only man with one left was Anderson.

Anderson had been the last to take off, when at 0228 hours he received a signal to divert to the Sorpe Dam. He had been on his way to the Diemel Dam, a gravity dam constructed in 1912 and holding 19.9 cubic metres of water. On route to the dam he came under heavy flak and the rear turret was damaged and put out of action. When he arrived at the Sorpe he found thick fog and after fifteen minutes he and the crew decided to return to base, taking with them the Upkeep bomb. He landed back at Scampton at 0530 hours with a number of the surviving crew agreeing he had, in the circumstances, done the right thing as they had no defences from the rear turret. But one comment was, 'in a hurry to get to bed.'

Gibson seemed to think that Anderson coming back with his bomb intact was a failure. It is alleged he made the comment, 'that he had been flying up and down the North Sea instead of going to the dams'. Others said this was made out of context and that as Anderson had only completed seven operations prior to arrival – of which two

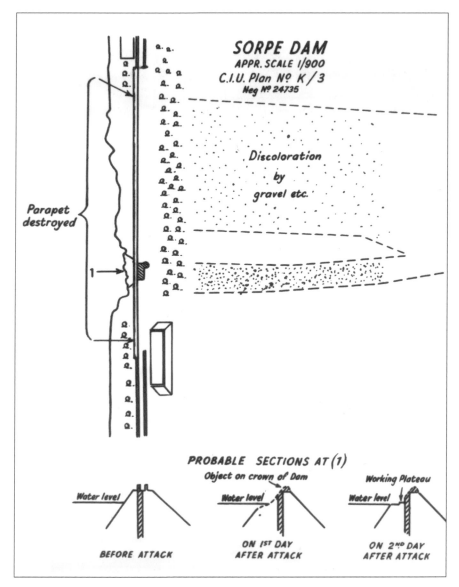

Sorpe Dam damage. © *National Archive*

were 'second dickie' when a new pilot flew with another crew to get experience – he and his crew should never have been posted to the squadron. Many of the crew on the raid were second tour men with a vast amount of experience and capable of such an operation. Whether Gibson knew this or chose to ignore it we shall never know. Of the five operations Anderson had completed as a captain, two were to Berlin and one to Duisburg in the Ruhr, so his opening operations would not have been easy ones.

Why did he bring the bomb back when he could have picked a suitable target to drop it on? One can only assume that being a special bomb and that he could not find the target, Anderson felt he must bring it back for future use. Whatever the situation there is no doubt that Anderson and his crew were treated very harshly and did not deserve to be treated in such a way.

Gibson was unforgiving and posted them back to 49 Squadron on 2 June.

Flight Sergeant Bill Townsend headed his aircraft 'O-Orange' towards the Ennepe Dam on the Schwelme River. It was early morning and the mist over the hills made navigation difficult, with the angle of the full moon making it look like a lake. The dam was finally spotted by the profile of the hill three-quarters of a mile away. He made three runs before the bomb aimer decided to let the bomb go at 0337 hours. It bounced once and exploded thirty seconds later. A high column of water came up from the explosion but there was no sign of damage to the dam. They signalled back at 0411 hours, ' Goner 58E'. 5 Group acknowledged back at 0412 hours.

(Author: There has been some controversy as to whether Townsend attacked the Ennepe Dam or the Bever Dam. Pilot Officer Lance Howard, Townsend's navigator, and the only officer in the crew, was, to the date of his passing, adamant that they had attacked the Ennepe Dam and not the Bever Dam. So, as he was there at the time, I am happy to go along with his version of events.)

On the return journey the sun was coming up on one side and the moon going down on the other. Because of high tension wires he kept the Lancaster right down on the deck at about 240 mph, it seemed to work as they had no opposition. They also flew back via the Mohne Dam and saw a sheet of water about seven miles long and four miles wide and it had reached the Emms Canal. When he reported back to Scampton of what he had seen at the Mohne he was not at first believed, but bomb aimer Charles Franklin confirmed what Townsend had seen and that he had seen houses sticking up above the fast moving water.

On reaching the enemy coast, he flew between Texel and Vlieland. The defences had a quick potshot at him, but he was not hit. The

German gunners had their guns so depressed their shells were bouncing off the water and over the top of the aircraft. As he flew over Holland oil was pouring from one engine, but he reached the English coast on three engines. He was spotted by the Observer Corps as he approached the English coast and they alerted a couple of fighter squadrons that it was two Heinkels flying in close formation. As they came in to land it seemed the whole station had come out to meet them. The cockpit windscreen was covered in oil and the landing was a heavy one. They landed at Scampton at 0615 hours, two hours after Gibson.

Because of a hearing loss, probably due to combat fatigue, Bill only flew two more operations and became a flying instructor on Wellingtons and finished the war a Flight Lieutenant, test-flying Lancasters in India. He did go back once to visit the Ennepe Dam.

As Townsend came down the ladder from his aircraft a voice asked him how it had gone. Being exhausted he brushed past the person asking the question and said, 'Wait till the debrief.' That person was no less than Air Chief Marshal Sir Arthur Harris, the Commander-in-Chief of Bomber Command.

Flight Sergeant George Chalmers, his wireless operator, was delighted with the reception by such top brass and shook hands all around, being congratulated on the clarity of his Morse code.

When Flight Lieutenant Martin had landed he was met by Barnes Wallis. When he saw the hole in the wing he was aghast, and when another damaged Lancaster landed the full impact of what the operation entailed suddenly struck him. He had, like most scientists, been so involved in the mechanics, that the practicality of carrying out the job and the cost had not hit him until now. When he learned of the losses he said to Micky Martin that if he had known he would never have started it. He once said that his greatest achievement in life was having four children and twenty grandchildren.

When the last signal was received, Harris decided to go to Scampton and meet those that had returned. By the time he arrived, Gibson, Shannon and Martin had landed.

As the Lancasters started to return, Leading Aircraftmen Law and Payne were waiting for Maudslay's aircraft 'J-Johnny', the crew got out full of high spirits. Les Knight, flying 'N-Nuts', said to Leading Aircraftman Keith Stretch, 'I hope I have not treated your engines too badly'. Corporal Chapman saw two Lancasters make awful landings, not one aircraft was without some form of damage and needed to be worked on before they could fly again. Of the eleven that came back, four were damaged; three by flak and one by machine-gun fire, probably from the dam itself. Gibson's 'G-George' had three small holes in its tail, which, bearing in mind the amount of time it had spent over the Mohne Dam, was remarkable. Also Rice's aircraft had considerable damage from hitting the water.

All the Lancasters that had returned were put into 'neutral', chocks put in place and the ground crews told to return at 0800 hours. But there were many empty pens where Lancasters had been only hours before. As time went on it was obvious they would never return, the only hope was that the crews had somehow baled out and had survived.

In the officers' mess, Edna Broxholme, who only a few hours earlier had served the crews with a supper of egg and bacon, looked at the many empty chairs. Morfydd Brooks, who worked in the sergeants' mess had seen them off and now came out to see them back. The roar of engines was heard, the first back was Flight Lieutenant Munro and then Pilot Officer Rice. The WAAF sergeant tried to calm them down making coffee and with the words, 'the rest won't be long now.' Then as more engines were heard they ran out to the landing strips and one by one more aircraft came in and landed. They were then told to go to the sergeants' mess to serve the first arrivals. But they waited and waited until the WAAF sergeant called them together and said, 'Of the nineteen aircraft, eight are missing and fifty-six of our young boys will never return'. They all burst into tears. As in the officers mess there were tables all laid up but empty. For days after they were all shattered by the losses, gradually things got back to normal, but nothing would be the same again.

Some months later Morfydd was posted to another squadron where she finished her service in the WAAFs. However, nothing would ever dim her memories of 617 Squadron, 'The Dambusters'.

When Gibson arrived back to his office in No. 2 Hangar he threw the detonation key which had armed his bomb to 'Chiefy' Powell. Powell kept it until his death in 1986, having had it mounted on a wooden wall plaque.

On the morning of 17 May 1943, Peggy Paterson, a WAAF driver, was parked outside the officers' mess and had seen the crews return and begin to party, not only for the success of the operation but for being alive to celebrate. They came out of the mess and poured beer all over the engine of her car.

CHAPTER 9

The Results

The BBC announced the following on the morning of 17 May 1943, read by news reader Frank Phillips:

This is London:

The Air Ministry have just released the following communique. In the early hours of this morning a force of Lancasters of Bomber Command led by Wing Commander Guy Gibson, DSO, DFC, attacked the Ruhr dams Mohne and Sorpe, reconnaissance showed the Mohne had been breached over a 100 yards and the power station swept away. Eight of the Lancasters are missing.

Mohne Dam breach. © Karl Schutte

Damage after breach

Water flowing from the Mohne dam breach

Village of Gunne after the Mohne dam breach

At dawn on 17 May, 1943, Dr Albert Speer, the Minister of Munitions, was landing at Werl, some distance from the Mohne Dam. He saw the damage done by the water to villages, towns and cities. The water had reached Kassel, thirty-five miles away from the Eder Dam, and the largest tank and aircraft engine manufacturing centre in Germany. At Wabern, two hundred yards of railway embankment had been destroyed; the station sidings at Kassel were starting to silt up and the dock railways under water, also parts of the U-boat, tank and artillery manufacturers had been affected. They were targets that Bomber Command had made at least ten attacks on, but not caused anything like the damage that the water had created.

He said that this was an attempt to strike at the whole armaments industry by destroying the hydroelectric plants of the Ruhr. He was given a report in the early hours of 17 May and found it most alarming.

The village of Gunne had been washed away and most of the town of Neheim-Husten. Here, Josef Greis risked his life to rescue children from an air raid shelter and raised the alarm, which saved many people from death. Johannes Kessler had heard the water in the distance and sent a comrade to an air raid shelter where 100 people were taking refuge and by his actions they also escaped. He then went on to houses where people were in shelters, and then with the

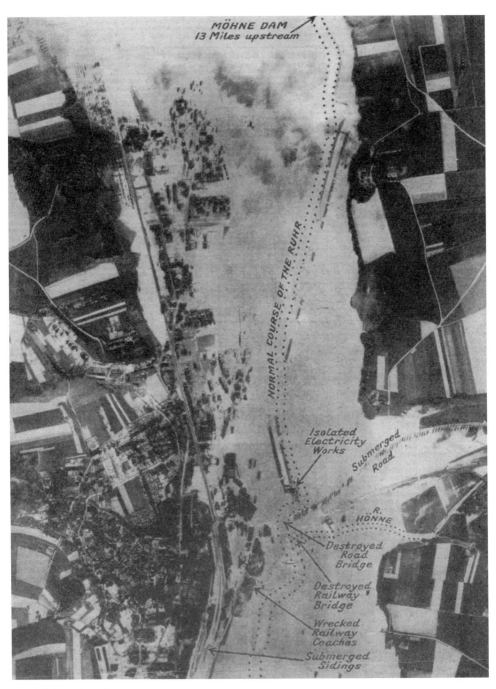

Mohne dam damage

The Mohne breach

Another shot of the breached Mohne dam

fire brigade and air defence workers, helped with clearance work. Both men were given a medal by the Mayor on 31 May 1943.

At Froenberg, the canal was destroyed, the power station put out of action and the railway bridge swept away as if it was matchwood. The main railway viaduct that joined Dortmund and Hagen was severed and thirty-two miles of countryside flooded.

Eder dam, after the attack

Eder dam breached

Dr Speer went on to the Sorpe Dam and ordered the pilot to land in open countryside near the dam, where two bombs had struck. (Author – When I interviewed Speer in 1980, he told me he had not realized how much damage water could do.)

Being a massive earth clay construction, the Sorpe could not be breached in the same way as the other two dams. When Speer arrived he was met by Mr Henning, the architect and engineer, who had been given the task of repairing the dam. Henning said that the repair of the Mohne Dam was not going to be an easy one as the breach was 250 feet at the top of the dam and 130 feet at the base. Over 134 million tons of water had poured out of the Mohne and 202 million tons out of the Eder.

Speer, having been told it was not going to be an easy job, telephoned for immediate anti-aircraft protection and that he wanted it in place that night. Within twenty-four hours Speer had sent a report to Hitler and 7,000 workers were sent to the Mohne Dam, all of them had been taken from Hitler's Atlantic Wall project, the workers would be accommodated in tents while carrying out the work. He brought in experts from all over Germany in order to restore water and electric supplies to the area affected. The figure of workers rose considerably as the repairs continued and Rommel was heard to say that one of the

Mohne dam being rebuilt, 1943

Damage after Mohne Dam breached. © *Norbert Kruger*

reasons for the lack of defences in the Normandy area was because of the amount of workers sent to rebuild the dams.

He is reported as saying that, 'the raid was a disaster for us for a number of months'.

The day after the raid, Goering and Goebbels arranged for the defences around the Sorpe Dam to be increased, whereas in fact, there had not been any defences at this dam.

Ken Brown found out after the war that if they had gone back the next night they would have been slaughtered. He was also told, when he visited the area, that the local schoolchildren were given the day off after the raid in 1943 to collect the dead fish to eat.

The bulk of the water at the Mohne had gone sixteen miles down the valley and from the Eder twenty miles.

At the end of May 1943, marshes and dykes about 100 miles away in Holland and Belgium were full of water. The locals recording that this was caused by the breached dams in the Ruhr.

On 16 May 1943, it was estimated that the Mohne had 132 million cubic feet of water behind it, on 18 May 1943 it was only 14.4 million.

A German report on 24 May 1943 showed the breach to be 76 metres wide and 21–23 metres deep and it was estimated it would take 2,000 men to repair it.

At the Sorpe, water was still seeping out into the basin. On 18 May 1943 a reconnaissance of the Ennepe showed damage caused by Townsend's bomb. It had been damaged over an area of 200 feet of its length. The upstream parapet which formed part of the concrete core, and the downstream parapet had disappeared. Repair to this dam was being carried out, and as described, with the greatest energy.

At the village of Hemelfonten, where everything was in ruins, the Pastor had read his last sermon on 16 May 1943. When the water struck he and the other villagers were in the cellar attached to the church and in the first wave of water the tower of the church could be seen but when the second came it disappeared out of sight. His body was later recovered from the ruins. The church collection taken on 16 May was not found until September 1945, along with wooden statues from the church and is now on display in a museum at Niederense. The site of the church can be seen today by the outline of its foundations. Where the chancel had been is a simple, large wooden cross.

In a cemetery at Affolden, there are thirteen graves, all with the date 17 May 1943. Three are for Gunter Neis, aged ten, Matilda Laborez, aged three, and Konrad Buttvher aged 74. They were all victims of the Eder Dam breach.

SS Colonel Burke, who was in charge of the rescue troops, said, 'The first impression of the damage is devastation'. The rescue work went on non-stop for about ninety hours. It was eight days before Burke's troops went back to their barracks. Thousands of cattle had to be dug out of the mud and buried. In the inland docks at Duisberg, shipping was ordered out into the Rhine. The Paul Baumer airfield, on the south band, was evacuated of all stores, equipment and aircraft. Neheim, fifty miles below the Mohne Dam was engulfed, swamping the town's coalfields and ironworks, forcing most of the 130,000 inhabitants to spend the night camping out on the high ground above the valley. In Neheim fifty-one men, sixty-six women and thirty children were lost. Forty houses destroyed and many damaged. Engineering plants making tank chassis, filters for wood generators and de-gassing cans were destroyed. Much of the livestock had been drowned.

In Dortmund there was flooding and every town and village between the Mohne and Duisburg had been affected by the flooding.

In all; 476 Germans were killed and sixty-nine missing. The other losses were Ukrainian, Dutch labourers, and French and Belgium PoW's, 593 killed and 156 missing.

Relief work went on until 25 May 1943, 1,843 troops were distributing drinking water in the Ruhr area where lines of water wagons and lines of people waited to be supplied with fresh water. All the rail and road bridges were damaged and repair to the Spitzen Power Station, which supplied 140,000 kW daily, took three weeks to repair. John Hopgood's bomb, which destroyed the power station at the Mohne Dam, had cut off electricity for the whole valley.

A number of works in the area of Hamm, Dortmund, Witten, Hahen and Gelsenkirchen were all out of action due to the water shortage. There was a loss of gas production of 50 per cent for several days.

A Swedish news reporter wrote:

> The flooding after the dams raid has created great havoc. The town of Soest had for a long time been like an island and entire buildings swept away. In Dortmund many streets were submerged and traffic restricted to flat bottom boats. The soldiers of the 1914/16 war were saying that not even the gunfire in Flanders had done more destruction than the British attack on the Ruhr.

At 1400 hours on 17 May 1943 a communiqué, issued by the German High Command, was picked up by the BBC Monitoring Service:

> Last night a force of Royal Air Force bombers penetrated Reich territory and dropped a small number of high explosives in several places. Two dams were damaged and the subsequent onrush of water caused many casualties among the civilian population, eight enemy aircraft were shot down ...

In Germany, Dr Joseph Goebbels, Adolf Hitler's director of propaganda, issued a news agency report claiming that the plan of the attack had been thought up by a Jew who had emigrated from Berlin. He also wrote a short news item for the newspapers, particularly the local papers in the flooded areas. The amount of damage caused was also published

However, only days later he said, 'The attacks of the British bombers on our dams in our valleys were very successful. The Fuhrer is exceedingly impatient and angry about the lack of preparedness on the part of our Luftwaffe. Damage to our production was more than normal.'

The death toll in Neheim alone was 147 Germans, 712 Russian and Poles and forty-one injured. In the Osterbir cemetery there are 479 Russian and Polish workers buried, forty PoW's, fifty-four French and a number of Dutch PoW's, who it was thought were working in the area of the flooding.

On the morning of 17 May 1943, two Spitfires flown by Flying Officers Searle and Efford from 542 PRU Squadron flew over the area and took photographs from 29,000 feet. Water was still seen flowing through the great gap in the Mohne Dam and the photographs showed the flood had reached a point sixteen miles down the valley. Two villages were under water, bridges had vanished, power stations and waterworks were isolated and railway communications disrupted. Efford saw mud deposits west of the Eder, along the Eder valley for up to twenty miles.

By late afternoon most of the water had drained away. Disruption to barge traffic on the Rhine was considerable, at one point the delay in the journey from Cologne to Holland amounted to six days. At the Sorpe Dam water was seen to be running down the face and carrying earth into the compensating basin.

On 18 May 1943, a further recce was made by 542 PRU Squadron, this time by Flying Officer Scott. His photographs and report found the lakes mostly drained away, hangars, barracks, ammunition dumps and landing grounds at Fritzler airfield submerged. It also showed that the Ennepe Dam had a minor breach, so Bill Townsend had in fact made an impact on the dam.

The reports of the attack were front page in *The Times*, the *Daily Telegraph*, *The Chronicle*, and *The Manchester Guardian* along with pictures of the breached Mohne Dam.

The Germans compiled a dossier on 617 Squadron, calling them the 'The Dam Raiders'; 'The Dambusters' and 'Gibson's Boys'.

Tony Burcher had been picked up by the Hitler Youth and taken to a local police station where they laid him on a wooden bed. By this time he was very thirsty and asked for a drink of water. This annoyed the corporal guarding him as he had to explain there was 'No Wasser' (water). Although he did not get a drink, Tony knew from this that the attack was a success. In his pocket was the stone the little boy had given him months earlier to drop on the Germans for killing his parents in an air raid. So far it had been a lucky charm and he had survived.

MOST SECRET   COPY NO 20

                                       T.O.O. 171610

ALCOVE NO. 266   Date: 17th May, 1943

_____

MOST IMMEDIATE

            Personal and Secret for Prime Minister from
Secretary of State for air.

            P.R.U. reports confirm success of upkeep.
Photos this morning show 200 foot breach in Möhne Dam,
disappearance of Power Station and widespread floods
reaching to Dortmund. While Eder Dam not yet photographed
Power Station one mile down stream has been under water
and very bad flooding has clearly taken place. Main
storage lake of reservoir appears drained. Sorpe Dam
being of different construction not expected to be
breached but crest damaged for 200 feet. Water flowing
over, seepage hoped for. Surprise was achieved and
weapon functioned admirably but attack involved very
accurate and low flying and our losses were 8 missing
out of 19 Lancasters despatched. Wing Commander Gibson
directed the operations by R/T and, after dropping his
weapon, flew around shooting at the flak. He returned
unscathed.

Top secret communique, post-raid © National Archives

On 20 December 1944, the German Intelligence Branch prepared a
report on the Mohne and Eder which gave an account of the raid on
the dam in May 1943 as seen by German eyes. It is shown to be
confused and inaccurate. It said that explosion No. 3 produced a
considerably smaller movement than 1, 2, and 4. Explosion 5 and 6

Headline in the Daily Telegraph *on the morning of 18 May*

Night after the raid; No. 5 Group Officers Mess, St Vincent's, Grantham, Lincolnshire. © *Wally Dunn (centre)*

were caused – according to the time and allowing for the distance –
by the mines dropped on the Eder Dam. It went on to describe the
torpedo netting that was fixed at about 25 metres from the water side
of the wall to floating buoys 350 metres apart. It consisted of two nets
six metres apart, and stretching down to a depth of 15 metres below
the edge of the overflow. At both sluice towers this distance was
ensured by floating wooden fenders 30 metres in length. The spot
where the mine struck the net could not be definitely established, but
it was assumed that the point of impact was near the left-hand sluice
tower looking down the valley, at a point where the floating fender is
badly damaged.

There is no doubt about the point of impact of the second mine,
which exploded near the left bank about 80 to 100 metres from the
wall. This caused the loose earth on the left bank to collapse over a
considerable distance. When the dam was emptied parts of this mine
were found.

The third bomb must have been dropped too late, as it went clean
over the wall and fell into an overflow pond situated below the dam
wall. This caused the destruction of a power plant built right across
the valley about 40 metres from the open side of the wall and it blew
up with a large sheet of flame. It also caused the electric in the whole
valley to fail. This also caused the roof of the left-hand sluice tower to
collapse and blew the gun posted there from the flat roof and out of
use. The crew in this tower then assisted the gun crew of the right-
hand sluice tower in carrying ammunition. At this time the road
across the dam was intact.

A fourth bomb was released and the wall between the two towers
collapsed and water poured into the valley.

The first bomb dropped on the Eder Dam exploded a considerable
distance from the wall, causing horizontal cracks on the whole centre
section of the wall, which was in any case thinner, right down to
the centre section of the wall. Whilst the second mine, which clearly
exploded nearer to the foot of the wall, caused a breach at a short
distance from the centre of the wall.

The raid on the Sorpe Dam was carried out on the same night, at
about 0045 hours, by a single aircraft from 20 metres. The dam was
not protected by anti-aircraft or balloon barrage or nets.

The aircraft flew several times across the dam in the direction of
the earth dam and did not release until the tenth run. This formed a

bomb crater on the water side of the earth wall close to the water line, covered only by 3 metres of water, with the result that it blanketed the explosion only to a minor degree, it took an upward direction and threw up a column of water to a height of 150 to 200 metres. The downward effect of the explosion was damped by the material of the rubble dam and explains why the effects of the explosion were not felt in Gottingen.

The people in the area went into a tunnel under the Sorpe Dam and when the bomb exploded the doors to the tunnel were blown off. If all five aircraft had attacked the Sorpe as planned there is some chance that even if it had not been breached, enough water would have gone down the valley to the armaments factories in the Ruhr Valley to render them useless.

A second attack was carried out on the Sorpe shortly after 0300 hours. Only one mine was dropped, it fell about 800 metres from the dam wall in the middle of the reservoir and did no damage.

Albert Speer said, 'We were in great danger, if the English had systematically destroyed all the dams in the region, our steel industry would have collapsed.'

At 0400 hours a State of Emergency was declared in Westphalia.

CHAPTER 10

Failed to Return

In the Second World War many airmen in Bomber Command had written in their flying logbook in red ink; 'Missing nothing further heard', 'Failed to return', or simply 'Missing'. This would be entered by their flight commander, who would inspect their logbooks every month to make sure their operations were entered accurately. Also when they had completed the required number of operations which

Date	Hour	Aircraft Type and No.	Pilot	Duty	REMARKS (Including results of bombing, gunnery, exercises, etc.)	Flying Times Day	Night
					URQUHART Time carried forward:	285·0	237·15
4/5/43	23·10	P	S/L MAUDSLAY	NAVIGATOR	TACTICS.		1·00
5/5/43	20·15	ED437	S/L MAUDSLAY	NAVIGATOR	X/C Nº 4.	2·40	
6/5/43	20·15	ED437	S/L MAUDSLAY	NAV.	X/C BOMBING. and TACT....		1·15
8/5/43	X. 1740		S/L MAUDSLAY	NAV.	RT. TEST.	1·00	
11/5/43	X 11·35		S/L MAUDSLAY	NAV.	EXERCISE.	4·05	
12/5/43	18·30	ED933	S/L MAUDSLAY	NAV.	EXERCISE		2·10
13/5/43	23·30	ED437	S/L MAUDSLAY	NAV.	X/C BOMBING, and TACTICS		3·2
14/5/43	19·15	Z.	S/L MAUDSLAY	NAV.	N.F.T. and BOMBING.	·20	
14/5/43	21·50	Z	S/L MAUDSLAY	NAV.	EXERCISE		3·4
16/5/43	22·00	Z.	S/L MAUDSLAY	NAV.	OPS. — EDER DAM MISSING.		
					TOTAL TIME....		

Logbook entry for Flying Officer Urquhart, Navigator to Maudslay.

would count as a tour, they were taken off operations for a rest period. On this occasion fifty-six flying logbooks were recorded in such a way.

Eight Lancaster aircraft and fifty-six men had failed to return.

Flying at such low-level there was little time to recover when hit by anti-aircraft fire, there was also the danger of hitting objects on the ground when flying so low.

The first casualty of the dams raid was Sergeant Vernon Byers, aged 32 and from Saskatchewan, Canada. He had taken off at 0930 hours and crashed at 1057 hours. On reaching the enemy coast he came under anti-aircraft fire from the island of Texel, it was here that Geoff Rice saw his Lancaster hit by gunfire when at 300 feet. It veered away off course and crashed into the sea near Vlieland Island, off the Frisian chain. The local authorities in the town of Den Heider, in the north of Holland, stated that a plane had come down east of the town between Texel and the Afsluitdijk, a large dyke that connected both parts of northern Holland. Byers and his crew; flight engineer Sergeant Alastair Taylor, aged 22, a former RAF Halton apprentice or Halton 'Brat' as they were known, his brother was a flight engineer in Bomber Command and survived the war; navigator Pilot Officer Jim Warner, aged 21; bomb aimer Sergeant Arthur Whittaker, his commission to Pilot Officer came through on 18 May 1943, and air gunners Sergeant Charles Jarvis, aged 21, and Sergeant James McDowell from Canada, he was the only one to be recovered from the sea at the Waddensee, by a vessel on 22 June 1943. He is now buried in the Harlington General Cemetery, The Netherlands; the remainder of the crew, including Byers, are remembered on the Runneymede Memorial. The Dutch record stated that the aircraft was hit by flak at 150 metres.

The second casualty was Flight Lieutenant Bill Astell, DFC, aged 23, and a very experienced pilot, having flown many operations in the Middle East. His Lancaster hit a high voltage cable near Dorsten airfield, Marbeck, on the outskirts of Borken, Germany. He and his crew; flight engineer Sergeant John Kinnear, aged 21; navigator Pilot Officer Floyd Wile, aged 24, from Nova Scotia, Canada; fellow Canadian, wireless operator Sergeant Abram 'Albert' Garshowitz; front gunner Sergeant Francis 'Frank' Garbas from Ontario; bomb aimer Flying Officer Donald Hopkinson; and rear gunner Sergeant Richard Bolitho from Northern Ireland. Astell and his crew were killed instantly and were buried at Borken, but post-war they were reburied in the Reichswald War Cemetery at Cleve.

Flight Lieutenant
Astell's grave
© *Alan Cooper*

Flight Lieutenant Robert Barlow, aged 32, from Carlton, Australia, crashed thirteen minutes after Astell, he also hit a cable. He had been the first to take-off from Scampton with his crew; flight engineer Sergeant Sam Whillis, aged 31, much older than the rest of the crew and the majority of the crews on the raid; navigator Flying Officer Phillip Burgess, aged 20, a young man to have a commission; wireless operator Flying Officer Charles Williams, DFC, an Australian from Queensland and again much older at 34; bomb aimer Sergeant Alan Gillespie, DFM, from Carlisle; front gunner Flying Officer Harvey Glinz, aged 22, from Winnipeg, Canada and lastly rear gunner Sergeant Jack Liddell, aged 18, from Axbridge, near Weston-Super-Mare and on his thirtieth operation. He had joined the RAF at the age of fifteen and half, under age of course, but looking older he managed to get

Part of the bulkhead from Barlow's aircraft. © *Chris Ward*

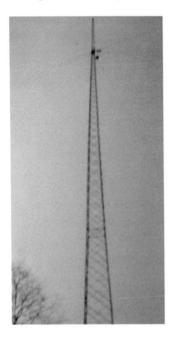

into the RAF, he was the youngest man on the Dambuster operation. All were killed, and, along with Astell's crew, are buried in the Reichswald War Cemetery.

The RAF Missing Research and Enquiry Unit found Barlow had crashed at Heeren-Herken-Haldern, south-east of Emmerich. A large bomb was found in the wreckage; it was taken away and defused for further research by the Luftwaffe. This was de-fused by Hauptmann Heinz Schweiger of the Luftwaffe Bomb Disposal Research Unit. At first the Germans thought this was a fuel tank, but within ten days draughtsman Siegfried Weiner had pro-duced drawings of the Upkeep bomb. Dr

The pylon which Barlow hit

F/Lt Barlow's grave.
© *Alan Cooper*

Reinhold Lambruch, the head of the Department Waffen Konstruction Luft, was asked to construct and develop an Uberwasserbombe (overwater bomb) and gave it the name Kurt. It was designed to be carried by an ME 262 jet fighter and later the FW 190 aircraft. The first bomb had a tail comprising of four fins but was later replaced by a box type biplane tail. It was never used, but by 1945 was given the go ahead by the German Air Ministry.

After the war the German report was sent to Barnes Wallis, he was not impressed, as although the report showed how it worked, no attempt had been made to forecast a full-scale performance from the model tests, he in fact said the report was useless.

The German report of the Upkeep bomb stated it was 3,900 kilograms (8,580lbs). A photograph of the bomb was taken by Herr Walter, leader of the railway police in the Reichsbahn-Director Wuupertal

(District Railway) and thought to have been taken at Dusseldorf-Kalkum, the base of the bomb disposal squad. When it was found, it had been buried 50cm into the ground.

Back in Canada Frank Garbas's mother never accepted his death, to her there was no body or a funeral, and she shared her tears and concerns with Albert Garshowitz's mother.

Some years after Frank's death, his nephew, Paul Morley promised his mother that if she could not visit his grave at the Reichswald Forest Cemetery, Kleve, Germany, then he would.

In 2000 he made that trip and met Bernie Siehling, who now lives in Grand Rapids, Michigan, but when he was 12-years-old he had been living in a farmhouse near Marbeck, Westphalia. He had seen ED 864-B, Astell's Lancaster, flying at treetop height over his farmhouse; it was on fire then flew away into the distance and exploded. The next day he cycled to the crash site, from where he saw the five bodies on the ground that had survived the crash, but not the subsequent fire. About 135 yards away was a huge crater. All the windows in the area had been broken by the blast. Near the crater was a statue to St Joseph, which was untouched! The Lancaster had struck a hydro-transmission pylon, sheared the tops off five poplar trees and then crashed in a farmer's field.

On his trip, Paul, along with five members of the Garshowitz family, visited the Mohne and Eder Dams. At the crash site they met Richard Siehling, Bernie's brother, he was a volunteer at the Raesfeld museum. He showed them around the museum and on the wall was a huge picture of the crashed ED 864-B, broken and burnt. He then took them to the spot where Paul's uncle had died.

They went on to the Borken City Cemetery where the crew of ED 864-B were first buried. From there to the Reichswald War Cemetery, a huge cemetery with the RAF personnel being buried to the left, the army personnel to the right and by regiment. As they arrived, his promise to his mother came flooding back. He soon found the seven graves and on top of Albert's grave were little pebbles, placed there by his family in the Jewish prayer of mourning. As promised to his sister Joan, Paul also put a small silver crucifix inside the engraved cross of the gravestone, also her photograph, taken with her uncle Frank the day he left Hamilton. He placed a wreath with a card saying, 'To my dear: I never met you, but I felt you in the tears of my mother. God bless you, Paul.'

The fourth aircraft lost was John Hopgood and his crew. How badly he had been wounded prior to the attack on the Mohne Dam we shall never know. Despite his injuries and those of his wireless operator John Minchin, as well as the possibility of Tony Burcher his front gunner being dead, he carried on in the best traditions of Bomber Command pilots and crews.

As has been stated previously,Tony Burcher was taken prisoner (No. 1341) and John Fraser was able to evade capture for ten days and managed to get to within thirty miles of the border before being captured. He spent seven days in Dulag Luft before being sent to Stalag Luft III at Sagan PoW No. 136 and was there when the Great Escape took place. He was one of the men known as penguins who daily distributed sand taken from the tunnels, by means of carrying it in bags in their trousers and walking about the camp slowly spreading the sand so it would not be noticed in one place.

Hopgood, aged 22; flight engineer Sergeant Charles Brennan; navigator Flying Officer Kenneth Earnshaw from Alberta, Canada; wireless operator Sergeant John Minchin, aged 26; front gunner Pilot Officer George Gregory, DFM, were all killed. Their bodies were taken to the local Luftwaffe base at Werl, by Alpine troops, then to Soest for burial, but after the war they were reburied at the Rheinberg War Cemetery, north of Krefeld. At the crash site today there is a wooden post with a plaque in brass on the top with an inscription.

Hopgood's crashed aircraft

In hindsight, there is no doubt that Hopgood should have at least been recommended or considered for a posthumous VC for his actions, or at least a Mention in Despatches, which, if not awarded the VC, is the only other award that could be awarded posthumously.

It was reported that a boy of twelve went to the Hopgood crash site and found a piece of charred triangular wood which he threw away. It was, it would appear, the bombsight that Fraser had used to line up the Mohne Dam. He did however keep the optical bombsight from the Lancaster.

Number five to go down was Pilot Officer Lewis Johnston Burpee, DFM, age 25, he also came from Canada, his son was born on Christman Eve 1943 and was also named Lewis Burpee, after the father he would never know. His cousin Matthew went missing on a raid on Rotterdam in 1941. His father, also called Lewis, had served in the Canadian Field Ambulance in France in the First World War.

It would appear that after crossing the coast near Roosendaal, Burpee turned to starboard and was caught by searchlights and light flak, the aircraft was soon on fire and crashed on the edge of the German night-fighter base at Gilze Rijen at 0153 hours. When his bomb went off many buildings on the airfield were destroyed and the airfield was out of action for some while, this in a way saved many a bomber crews' lives. The damage was also a big financial blow to the Germans. Ken Brown, following both Burpee and Ottley, saw them crash shortly before he was told to go to the Sorpe Dam.

Burpee and his crew; flight engineer Sergeant Guy Pegler, aged 21; navigator Sergeant Tom Jaye, aged 20, who had trained as a pilot but being short became a navigator and trained with Pan Am Airways in Miami, Florida; wireless operator Pilot Officer Len Weller, aged 27; bomb aimer Sergeant James Arthur, aged 25, from Ontario, Canada, and the two air gunners Sergeant Bill Long, age 19, and Sergeant Joe Brady, age 27, another Canadian from Alberta, Canada, were all instantly killed. At the time they were all buried at Prinsen Lage, two miles from Breda, Holland and in 1948 they were reburied in Bergen-op-Zoom Cemetery, Holland.

The sixth to go down was Pilot Officer Warner Ottley, DFC, at 0235 hours. He went down to anti-aircraft fire north of Hamm. In a German newspaper there was a photograph of Ottley's aircraft with a caption underneath which said: 'The end of a murder plane. This Lancaster bomber will not return to England after its slight intrusion against German territory.' He crashed at Boselagerschen

Ottley crash site

Wald in Heessen, in a forest. He and his crew; flight engineer Sergeant Ronald Marsden, aged 21; navigator Flying Officer Jack Barrett, DFC, also 21, he did not live to know he had been awarded the DFC; wireless operator Sergeant Jack Guterman, DFM, age 22, he had flown a remarkable fifty-four operations, thirty-eight as a mid-upper gunner and sixteen as a wireless-operator, so although only wearing one, he was entitled to two flying brevets on his left breast; bomb aimer Sergeant Tommy Johnston; and the front gunner Sergeant Harry Strange, aged 20. The rear gunner, Sergeant Freddie Tees, age 20, survived to be a prisoner of war. The site of the crash has been tended by a German couple for over twenty years.

Number seven to be shot down was the B Flight Commander, Squadron Leader Henry Maudslay, DFC; he was shot down at about the same time as Ottley. He crashed after being damaged over the Mohne Dam and then hit again by anti-aircraft fire at Klein-Netterden, all were killed and taken to Dusseldorf for burial. After the war, as with many aircrew, they were reburied in designated war grave sites such as the Reichswald.

Maudslay was thirty-one, his crew was; flight engineer Sergeant John Marriott, DFM, age 22, his sisters received his DFM from the King at Buckingham Palace; navigator Flying Officer Robert Urquhart, DFC, from Canada, he also did not live to receive his DFC; wireless operator Sergeant Allan Cottam, age 30, and from Alberta, Canada; bomb aimer Pilot Officer Mike Fuller, age 22, and squadron gunnery leader Flying Officer Bill Tytherleigh, DFC, age 20, his DFC was for forty-four operations, but again he did not live to receive it; Sergeant Norman Burrows was the other air gunner in Maudslay's crew, which was a very experienced crew. At first they were buried in Dusseldorf North Cemetery but later moved to the Reichswald War Cemetery.

The eighth and final aircraft lost was Squadron Leader Henry 'Dinghy' Young, DFC, aged 27. Having survived a number of ditchings where dinghies were involved it was ironic that his final ending was again in the sea. He had been hit by flak west of Amsterdam and his aircraft crashed in flames into the sea just off the Dutch coast between Ymuiden and Castricum. It was said the aircraft was too far to the south and that flying low was his downfall, as a flak position between the sand dunes at Ymuiden was able to shoot him down. This was the start of his third tour of operations.

'Dinghy' Young's crashed aircraft

Born in Belgravia, London, he spent much of his life in the USA. His father served in the 4th Battalion of the Queen's Royal West Surrey Regiment. He came back to England, to Oxford, where he attended Trinity College to read law. He was No. 2 in the Oxford crew that beat Cambridge in the last boat race before the war, winning by two lengths. He spent quite a bit of his flying in the Middle East with 104 Squadron. While there he took part in attacks on Naples, Tripoli, Brandish, and other targets such as airfields at Castel Benito. When awarded a bar to his DFC he had flown fifty-one operations.

In 1943 he joined 57 Squadron on Lancasters, where he had flown Wellingtons previously. When he joined 617 Squadron he had flown seventy-nine operations and was chosen by Gibson to be his second in command.

His flight engineer was Sergeant David Horsfall, age 23, from Hove in Sussex; the navigator, Sergeant Charles Roberts, from Cromer in Norfolk, was a newcomer to the crew; wireless operator Sergeant Lawrence Nichols, age 32, from Kent; bomb aimer, Flying Officer Vincent MacCausland, age 30, was from Canada; the front air gunner, Sergeant Gordon Yeo, aged 21, from South Wales, and the rear gunner, Sergeant Wilfred Ibbottson, age 28, was from West Yorkshire.

The body of Sergeant Gordon Yeo was washed up near Wyk-aan-Zee on 27 May. All are buried at Bergen General Cemetery.

Of the 133 that set off from Scampton, thirty were from Canada and six from Alberta, of these fourteen were killed and one was a PoW. Four of the men from Canada who returned from the raid were later killed in the war.

Of the fifty-three who were killed, twenty-seven are buried in the Reichswald War Cemtery, Young and his crew of six are buried in Bergen General War Cemetery, five in the Rhineberg War Cemetery, seven in the Bergen-Op-Zoom War Cemetery, one in the Harlington War Cemetery and six are remembered on the Runnymede War Memorial.

CHAPTER 11

Post Dams

As ordered, the ground crew reported for duty at 0800 hours on 17 May 1943.

At 1000 hours all ranks were ordered to the mess hall where they met Wing Commander Guy Gibson who said, 'Last night we went out and altered the map.' He gave an edited account of the raid and the targets, then thanked them all and told them to proceed to the guardroom where they would be given a three-day leave pass. The aircrew received seven days leave.

The Dams party, June 1943, Guy Gibson signs the photograph of the Mohne Dam breach

Gibson stayed behind writing the next of kin letters, helped by Sergeant Jim Heveron.

Before he went on leave, Les Munro was asked by Gibson what had happened and why he had to return early. When Munro told him, he said, 'You were flying too high' and walked away.

However, for Cyril Anderson and his crew, it would appear that coming back with his bomb and not being able to find the target was unacceptable to Gibson, so he sent Anderson and his crew back to 49 Squadron.

It was alleged that Gibson made a comment that Anderson, 'Flew up and down the North Sea all night on the Dams raid.' Others have said this was taken out of context, as although a crew had only a few operations under their belt, they had undergone operations to heavily defended targets before and when they returned to 49 Squadron they completed another twenty-odd operations, again on heavily defended targets. He is, of course, recorded on the 617 Squadron memorial at Woodhall Spa. In hindsight, to ask a crew with only five operations as a crew to take part in the dams' raid was ridiculous, many of the crews were second tour men and had a wealth of experience under their belt. It would appear that either Gibson did not know this, or refused to accept that he was asking too much of a crew who did their best, but did not have the experience needed.

Did Gibson know that Anderson and his crew had only flown five operations when they arrived at 617 Squadron? If he had, maybe he would have been a little more sympathetic and put himself in Anderson's shoes, let's hope so.

Cyril had joined the RAF as a fitter in 1934. He was born in Wakefield and underwent an apprenticeship with the British Jeffery Diamond Company in Wakefield. His service took him to Singapore and Seletar. When the Second World War began he went for flying training in Canada, with 33 SFTS, received his flying wings on 2 January 1943 and joined 49 Squadron on 23 February 1943. Sadly, as well as coping with his flying duties, his baby son died in 1943. He was named Graham Thorpe Anderson.

It would appear that prior to the dams raid, Gibson had returned two crews to their squadrons as 'Failing to meet the required standard'. One other crew had decided to leave of their own free will because Gibson regarded the navigator as not suitable.

A message was sent by Air Chief Marshal Harris to the Air Officer Commanding 5 Group, he sent them his warmest congratulations for the way they had carried out the operations and said it was a major victory in the Battle of the Ruhr.

The Secretary of State for Air, Sir Archibald Sinclair, gave out the news and sent a telegram to HQ Bomber Command congratulating Gibson and his squadron on behalf of the War Cabinet. He called the raid, 'A Trenchard blow for victory.'

Lord Trenchard sent his congratulations, 'The wonderful work of Bomber Command is being recognized now.'

Sir Charles Portal, the Chief of the Air Staff, sent his congratulations to Harris. Being against the idea of the raids at first, but being the man he was. Harris sent a telegram to Barnes Wallis in which he said that, but for his knowledge, skill and persistence, the efforts of the crews would have been in vain. 'We,' he said, 'in Bomber Command, owe everything to you.'

Harris was summoned to meet the King at Buckingham Palace; here His Majesty expressed his personal congratulations for the Command's recent exploits and in particular the success of the raid on the dams. Harris explained that, 'None of us had any idea what this project was; we were just given instructions to construct and modify various items. The head of the programme was Dr Barnes Wallis.'

General Eaker, the commander of the US Eight Air Force sent a message to Harris congratulating them from the American Air Forces.

Barnes Wallis described the men of 617 Squadron as, 'Incomparable Young Men.'

Messages came from the Air Officer Commanding Coastal Command, 'Well done 5 Group and Scampton. A magnificent night's work, Lessor.'

From the Air Officer Commanding Fighter Command, 'Heartiest congratulations from all in Fighter Command on your magnificent exploit in wrecking the Mohne and Eder Dams. Probably the greatest and most far-reaching destruction yet wreaked on Germany in a single night. Leigh-Mallory.'

A reconnaissance flight sent from RAF Benson showed the breach in the dams. The *Daily Telegraph* headline was, 'RAF Blow Up, Three Key Dams in Germany'. The *Daily Mirror* had the title, 'The Smash-Up: RAF Picture Testifies to Perfect Bombing'. Another newspaper said, 'Pilot Sees Breach in Dam by Moonlight.' In Canada the *Winnipeg Free Press* had a lead page of, 'Vast areas of the Reich are flooded.' In *Baltimore News – Press*, 'Rioting after Dam Break thousands drown in Ruhr.'

Numb. 36030   2361

SUPPLEMENT
TO
The London Gazette
Of TUESDAY, the 25th of MAY, 1943

Published by Authority

Registered as a newspaper

FRIDAY, 28 MAY, 1943

Air Ministry, 28th May, 1943.

ROYAL AIR FORCE.

The KING has been graciously pleased to confer the VICTORIA CROSS on the under-mentioned officer in recognition of most conspicuous bravery:—

Acting Wing Commander Guy Penrose GIBSON, D.S.O., D.F.C. (39438), Reserve of Air Force Officers, No. 617 Squadron:—

Air Ministry, 28th May, 1943.

ROYAL AIR FORCE.

The KING has been graciously pleased to approve the following awards in recognition of gallantry displayed in flying operations against the enemy:—

On the night of 16th May, 1943, a force of Lancaster bombers was detailed to attack the Moehne, Eder and Sorpe dams in Germany. The operation was one of great difficulty and hazard, demanding a high degree of skill and courage and close co-operation between the crews of the aircraft engaged. Nevertheless, a telling blow was struck at the enemy by the successful breaching of the Mohne and Eder dams. This outstanding success reflects the greatest credit on the efforts of the following personnel who participated in the operation in various capacities as members of aircraft crew.

Distinguished Service Order.

Flight Lieutenant Joseph Charles McCARTHY, D.F.C. (Can/J.9346), Royal Canadian Air Force, No. 617 Squadron.

Flight Lieutenant David John Hatfield MALTBY, D.F.C. (60335), Royal Air Force Volunteer Reserve, No. 617 Squadron.

Acting Flight Lieutenant Harold Brownlow MARTIN, D.F.C. (68795), Royal Air Force Volunteer Reserve, No. 617 Squadron.

Acting Flight Lieutenant David John SHANNON, D.F.C. (Aus. 407729), Royal Australian Air Force, No. 617 Squadron.

Pilot Officer Leslie Gordon KNIGHT (Aus.401449), Royal Australian Air Force, No. 617 Squadron.

Bar to Distinguished Flying Cross.

Acting Flight Lieutenant Robert Claude HAY, D.F.C. (Aus.407071), Royal Australian Air Force, No. 617 Squadron.

Acting Flight Lieutenant Robert Edward George HUTCHISON, D.F.C. (120854), Royal Air Force Volunteer Reserve, No. 617 Squadron.

Acting Flight Lieutenant Jack Frederick LEGGO, D.F.C. (Aus.402367), Royal Australian Air Force, No. 617 Squadron.

Flying Officer Daniel Revil WALKER, D.F.C.

(Can/J.15330), Royal Canadian Air Force, No. 617 Squadron.

Distinguished Flying Cross.

Acting Flight Lieutenant Richard Dacre TREVOR-ROPER, D.F.M. (47354), No. 617 Squadron.

Flying Officer Jack BUCKLEY (129460), Royal Air Force Volunteer Reserve, No. 617 Squadron.

Flying Officer Leonard CHAMBERS (N.Z.403758), Royal New Zealand Air Force, No. 617 Squadron.

Flying Officer Harold Sydney HOBDAY (119929), Royal Air Force Volunteer Reserve, No. 617 Squadron.

Flying Officer Edward Cuthbert JOHNSON (119126), Royal Air Force Volunteer Reserve, No. 617 Squadron.

Pilot Officer George Andrew DEERING (Can/J.17245), Royal Canadian Air Force, No. 617 Squadron.

Pilot Officer John FORT (49575), No. 617 Squadron.

Pilot Officer Cecil Lancelot HOWARD (Aus.406248), Royal Australian Air Force, No. 617 Squadron.

Pilot Officer Frederick Michael SPAFFORD, D.F.M. (Aus.403380), Royal Australian Air Force, No. 617 Squadron.

Pilot Officer Harlo Torger TAERUM (Can/J.16688), Royal Canadian Air Force, No. 617 Squadron.

Conspicuous Gallantry Medal (Flying).

Can/R.94567 Flight Sergeant Kenneth William BROWN, Royal Canadian Air Force, No. 617 Squadron.

656738 Flight Sergeant William Clifford TOWNSEND, D.F.M., No. 617 Squadron.

Bar to Distinguished Flying Medal.

1165320 Sergeant Charles Ernest FRANKLIN, D.F.M., No. 617 Squadron.

Distinguished Flying Medal.

552201 Flight Sergeant George Alexander CHALMERS, No. 617 Squadron.

Can/R.112723 Flight Sergeant Donald Arthur MACLEAN, Royal Canadian Air Force, No. 617 Squadron.

Aus.408076 Flight Sergeant Thomas Drayton SIMPSON, Royal Australian Air Force, No. 617 Squadron.

655673 Flight Sergeant Leonard Joseph SUMPTER, No. 617 Squadron.

919764 Sergeant Dudley Percy HEAL, No. 617 Squadron.

1199666 Sergeant George Leonard JOHNSON, No. 617 Squadron.

1144183 Sergeant Vivian NICHOLSON, No. 617 Squadron.

Can/R.114949 Sergeant Stefan OANCIA, Royal Canadian Air Force, No. 617 Squadron.

652403 Sergeant John PULFORD, No. 617 Squadron.

1381334 Sergeant Edward WEBB, No. 617 Squadron.

1517241 Sergeant Raymond WILKINSON, No. 617 Squadron.

The commendations, as printed in The London Gazette, *25th May, 1943*

The Air Ministry publicity department sent down a photographer who took pictures of the crew, not in black and white, but colour.

On 27 May 1943, a letter was sent to the Secretary of State in regard to the attack on the breaching of the Ruhr dams.

Owing to the attacks on the German dams, some concern was being shown for the UK dams, of which several were vital and unprotected. The most important one was Loch Ericht, the Rannoch end of this dam held more water than the Mohne Dam. If breached, the Scottish Power Company contributions to the grid would be at an end. There was also Kinlochleven Blackwater dam; if this was breached about 3,000 operatives of the British Aluminium Company would be swamped. Then came the Laggan dam, if this was breached, the British Tunnel and the Scottish power dam at Dunalastair would be lost.

In Germany on 17 May 1943, Karl Schutte was still at his post on what was left of the Mohne Dam. He said that an observer plane went over, which they fired upon. His gun and accommodation was like a rubbish dump. Everything was riddled with bullets. A General arrived by small aircraft and presented the defenders with the Iron Cross. On the following day Generaloberst Weise arrived, he was the head of all air force units. He went on to say that they had done their best, and that they had shot down one aircraft. After that Karl and his comrades felt very proud that they had been a part of the attack.

Defences around the Mohne Dam after the attack

Mohne being re-built, 1943

The defences at the dams were strengthened. A Captain Lose, of the German army, was given the task of devising water defences,

(a) *Guns*
6 × 8.8 cm flak
6 × 7.5 cm flak
4 × 2 cm flak

(b) *Rockets*
Eleven multiple rocket guns capable of firing fifteen rounds simultaneously.

(c) *Smoke*
Smoke defences consisted of about 300 smoke generators, hand operated at about 150 metre intervals on the dam itself and around the S.E.E. Some were operated on the S.E.E. from boats.

(d) *Balloons*
In addition to the twenty small balloons, another thirty-five large balloons were employed; the whole fifty-five balloons forming a defensive ring around the dam. Some were anchored on buoys and some were anchored on the S.E.E. by boats.

(e) *Underwater Defences*
   (i)   Immediately on the water side of the dam were situated large baulks of timber, interconnected by chains, and with their upper ends held at water level by groups of ten buoys. These buoys were in turn held in position by connecting logs.

   (ii) The submerged end of the logs were about 20 metres distance from the base of the dam, and were fitted with firm buoys and attached to them, boxes filled with sand and concrete. These boxes, by their weight, held the ends of the logs under the water. If the sand and concrete is emptied from the boxes, the submerged ends were brought to the surface by the buoys. This could be done at will, for example, when repairs had to be carried out. The logs formed an underwater stockade to prevent an explosion at the base of the dam itself.

(iii) Three rows of steel mesh were located about 100 metres to the east of the dam, strengthened under water from shore to shore. They are held at water level by buoys which are anchored at both shores, by steel wires.

(f) *Sea Mine Defences*
Consisted of wire barrages of mines, totalling twenty-two mines.

1st Barrage – 450 metres from the dam and parallel with it, consisting of ten mines in all.

2nd Barrage – 650 metres from the dam and parallel with it, consisting of six mines in all.

3rd Barrage – 250 metres west of the Deslk Bridge, consisting of six mines running parallel with the bridge.

These were designed to guard the dam against low flying aircraft from the east.

(g) *Above Water Defences*
A cable 450 metres long stretched from shore to shore fixed by two pylons 85 metres high.

At the Eder Dam area the SS Flak-Company was extended into Arolsen and in March 1941 they moved into the SS-Barracks in Unna, but after a few months they were returned to Arolsen. In December 1941 came the formation of a SS-Flak-Reserve-Regiment. At the same time an order came out that the SS-Police-Flak-Reserve Battery should be disbanded. To replace it was a Reserve Regiment, consisting of the following: two batteries of 8.8cm guns and 3.7cm guns, but up to May 1943 this had not been finalized and only consisted of 3.7cm guns at Warburg and 2.0cm at Sherdede.

At the Sorpe Dams, three light batteries and a balloon carrier were installed, also a fog unit (Nebel) remained until December 1943. At the Eder, two light batteries, each with twelve 2cm guns, one train with four 3.7cm and two batteries each with four 8.8cm guns. Also twenty-four low-level and twenty-four high-level balloons, the latter chained, as well as one Schiekarron batteerie (mobile lumber battery), a fog unit and a rifle company.

On 23 September 1943, the breach in the Mohne Dam was filled.

On 22 October 1943 the dam, including the upper covering of reinforced concrete, was ready. The adjoining plants, such as the power stations, the regulating basin and the bridges were left untouched, but the damming up of water in the reservoir could begin again, after a summer with ample rain.

Both Speer and Wallis were in agreement that the chance was missed to make sure the dams were not repaired, the scaffolding etc. was only made of wood, so would have not withstood conventional bombs.

When the alarm was first raised at Arolson to the SS-Flak-Reserve-Regiment, Oberleutnant Saahr received a call at 0132 hours that, 'Several airplanes are circling over the Eder Valley Dam.' He contacted the 3rd Home Guard Battalion in Hemfurth, here they confirmed that three planes were over the lake and the dam. At 0150 hours a second call confirmed the situation and that the planes were dropping light flares and had switched on their searchlights. Oberleutnant Saahr reported this to the SS-Flak-Reserve.

At 0225 hours the Army Base Command ordered a rescue group of thirty men to the dam site. In the meantime the force of the escaping water had taken other parts of the wall and 8500cu.m. per second poured through the 70m wide and 22m high hole.

At the barracks lorries assembled and took the men to the dams area. At first it was thought that commandos had landed to destroy the dam, live ammunition was issued and the order 'Load and safety' was given.

They found houses under water and animal carcasses. At 0500 hours the first column of a 120 men of the SS-Flak-Reserve Regiment arrived. People were standing on the Hamlet at Hemfurth and a chain was formed to try and get them down by means of a road higher up. A boat manned by SS. Uf Dorschuk raced by, paddling madly, he was able to reach the calmer waters behind the ruins and the people were rescued.

From the fire stations men from the areas were called out, all were under the order of the Commander and his men of the SS Flak Regiment. To see the damage SS. St Burk travelled with the Transport Commander Herrn Brauner to the affected area. He did not return until 1000 hours and he split the whole area into two sections. As well as the firemen the police were also involved. It was an awful sight, with dead animals still chained up in their stables. By 1400 hours the water had subsided by 28cm.

On 18 May 1943, the number of men involved in the rescue had risen to 600. The SS men were jumping into the water and roping up the dead animals in buildings to drag them out and in some cases buildings had to be blasted away to get at dead animals. Provisions were also made to establish a bridge in the area at Affolden-Mehlen.

All access to the area of the Eder Dam was prevented, damaged areas were closed and all cameras and film was confiscated and the owners taken away. At Hemfurth a temporary ferry was established. The main problem was drinking water and fuel for motor vehicles was also running low.

On the 21 May, many of the SS men had been working for over ninety hours and their uniforms were stuck to them, another task for the SS was digging graves for the dead. Coffins were covered in flags and flowers. Only the work by the troops enabled the burials to take place. It was 1500 hours on 21 May 1943 when the bodies were interred with military honours in cemeteries at Affolden, Hemfurth, Mehlen, and Bergheim.

At Affolden the church was full, the front row was full with relatives of the dead, including soldiers who had been recalled from the front to attend. For the next two days the work continued. The last day was on 24 May 1943, a week since the dams were attacked. The soldiers went back to their barracks and those that had made special efforts were awarded the Iron Cross. On 26 May 1943 the SS-Flak-Reserve-Regiment resumed its normal function and in July 1943 moved to Munchen and remained there until the end of the war.

The reconstruction of the Eder Dam was made harder because a number of markers had been swept away by the floods, or severely damaged. Those that remained were no longer able to register the abnormal water masses. For this reason there were only a few certain marker observations available for the Mohne and upper Ruhr. Only from the middle of the Ruhr Valley, downriver from Hagen, was regular and accurate metering possible, although the height of the flood water was obvious from the signs on the land.

On 27 May 1943 the King and Queen visited RAF Scampton. They came by road and went to the officers' mess for lunch. Photographs of some of the crews were taken with the royal party. After lunch in the officers' mess they went to inspect the aircraft of 617 and 57 Squadrons, also the air and ground crews.

At the presentation to Wing Commander Guy Gibson, Squadron Leader David Maltby, Flight Lieutenants Micky Martin and Les Munro, Flight Sergeant Ken Brown and Flight Lieutenant Joe McCarthy also had pictures taken with the royal couple.

In No. 2 Hangar they were shown photographs of the breached dams, also the models of the dams. It was here that the squadron mottos and coat of arms was submitted to the King by Gibson. However, the decision was delayed until the Chester Herald, an officer of arms at the College of Arms in London, had been consulted. Doctor Barnes Wallis also explained how the bomb worked.

The King meets Les Munro

McCarthy, Les Knight, Dave Shannon, and Sidney Hobday during a visit from the Royal couple

The Royal Visit outside Officers Mess, RAF Scampton.

On 19 May 1943, Gibson was recommended for the Victoria Cross by Air Chief Marshal Sir Arthur Harris. This showed he had flown 241 hours on Hampdens at the beginning of the war, 199 hours on fighters, and 200 hours on Lancasters. A full two page recommendation was submitted to the King on 22 May 1943 by the Secretary of State and on 23 May 1943 Gibson's logbook read, 'Awarded VC'.

As well as Gibson's award, there were thirty-three other awards; five DSO's, four bars to the DFC, ten DFC's, two CGM's and a bar to the DFM, which turned out to be the only one awarded to 617 Squadron in the Second World War, and eleven DFM's. Flight Sergeant Vivian Nicholson was awarded the DFM for this, his first operation.

Guy Gibson, VC

Guy Gibson, VC, Les Knight, Mick Martin on right and Maltby on left

Guy Gibson had been troubled with a painful carbuncle before the raid and afterwards had gone into RAF Rauceby, a military hospital, to have it lanced. While there he asked a WAAF nurse, a Mrs Backhurst, who worked in the operating theatre, if she could take his tunic to the hospital tailor to have the Victoria Cross ribbon sewn on. The tailor said it would be an honour to sew the highest decoration in the country on his tunic and he would return it in person.

In early June 1943 awards were announced to the ground crew of 617 Squadron. These were made by Gibson and endorsed by Group Captain Charles Whitworth, the Station Commander at RAF Scampton. Flight Lieutenant Caple, Pilot Officer Watson, Warrant Officer Taylor, Sergeant Chambers, Flight Sergeants Smith, Gover, and Campbell, all were engineers, armourer fitters or instrument makers on the squadron. Wing Commander Wally Dunn, the Chief Signal's Officer at 5 Group; Wing Commander Brown, 5 Group Engineering Officer; Squadron Leader Goodwin, 5 Group Armaments Officer; plus Group Captain Satterly and Group Captain Whitworth himself, were all awarded Commendations for Meritorious Service, but as was said before, nothing for Flight Sergeant George Powell or Sergeant Jim Heveron.

Flight Lieutenant David Maltby was promoted to Squadron Leader and given command of A Flight, taking the place of 'Dinghy' Young, sadly lost on the raid.

On 11 June 1943, repairs to the Eder began, huts were installed, stores and material assembled, and two light bridges thrown across the Eder.

On 19 June 1943, Gibson went to Maidstone for a Wings for Victory event, at the end there was a fly-past by four Lancasters, flown by Maltby, Shannon, Mick Martin and Munro.

On 21 June 1943, the aircrew that were to be decorated for the dams raid left Lincoln Station by train to London. The party consisted of forty-five men; some were not to be decorated but would attend the after party.

The big day came on 22 June 1943, at 1015 hours. The King had gone to North Africa for two weeks to visit the troops after the battle of El Alamein and on 20 June went on HMS *Aurora* to visit the island of Malta. On 15 April 1942, he had awarded the island the George Cross and said as soon as it was possible he would visit the island. Therefore, it was a surprise when the Queen – later the Queen Mother – took the investiture. This was the first time since Queen Victoria that a Queen had presided over an investiture. She was hatless and wore a spray of roses on her dress. Accompanying the Queen was the Lord Chamberlain, Lord Clarendon, Lady Delia Peel and other members of the Royal Household.

It was normal for anyone awarded the VC to be presented last, but on this occasion it was Wing Commander Guy Gibson who walked up first to receive his award of the VC and the bar to his DSO, awarded at the end of his tour with 106 Squadron. At the time, this made Gibson the most decorated member of the Royal Air Force in the Second World War. The Lord Chamberlain read out the citation for Gibson's VC and described it as one of the most devastating attacks of the war.

The Queen asked Gibson if he had all his 'fellow raiders' with him, he said he had one missing. His flight engineer, Sergeant John Pulford, was sick at the time and was not presented with his DFM until 16 November 1943, this time by the King.

Also decorated at the same time was Roy Chadwick, the designer of the Lancaster which had carried the 'bouncing bomb', he was awarded the CBE. Many photographs were taken at the time outside Buckingham Palace. Gibson left by a side entrance, with few people seeing him go, but later he was interviewed by the *Daily Mirror* in his West End hotel. Sadly, it would have been the nineteenth birthday of Jack Liddell; he was killed on the raid.

That evening A.V. Roe put on a dinner in the Hungarian Rooms, Dorland House, Lower Regent Street; now the Standard Charter Bank. The menu for the dinner had the incorrect title 'Damn Buster', the corrected version 'Dambusters' stuck to this day. The music for the evening was provided by the famous band leader Jack Hylton.

A large photograph of the breached Mohne Dam was signed – in the breach itself – by Gibson, the remainder signed on the right-hand side of the breach. This was then presented to Barnes Wallis, and today resides in the exhibition devoted to Barnes Wallis with a presentation of his working office. Gibson himself was presented with a model – in silver – of a Lancaster bomber by A.V. Roe. Gibson commented at the time of the presentation, 'The success of the attack on the dams was due to hundreds of technicians, and above all, to the Air Officers Commanding in the Group and the Senior Staff Officer. We flying crews are indebted to them all.'

The following day the Secretary of State for Air visited Scampton, but as Gibson was away, Harlo Taerum reconstructed the raid for him, he then went on two weeks leave. He told Gibson he was going to South Wales for his leave, upon which Gibson fixed him up to give a Wings for Victory speech at Bridgend, South Wales.

In Calgary, Harlow's mother went to the cinema with her other son Lorne – who was later also to be killed flying with the RAF in the UK – and saw the presentation of medals at Buckingham Palace. She saw her son presented with his DFC, they were guests of Capital Theatre.

On 17 July 1943, the Eder was now fully drained. A light railway had been constructed over one of the bridges (seen on 11 June 1943) to the foot of the dam; there were now fourteen huts in the area of the dam.

On 20 July 1943, Gibson and his wife Eve were invited to spend a weekend at Chequers as guests of Prime Minister Winston Churchill and Mrs Churchill. On 21 July 1943 they were picked up at the Ritz Hotel where they had spent the night and taken to Chequers by car.

On 2 August 1943, he again took part in an operation, flying with the new commanding officer Squadron Leader George Holden, DFC; the target was a flying bomb site at de Cassan in France.

In August, he was invited again by Churchill to make a goodwill tour of the USA and Canada, its official title was to be a lecture tour for the Ministry of Information. He left London on 4 August bound for the Clyde, where he boarded the *Queen Mary*, not a liner in wartime, but a troopship. With him, besides Churchill, Mrs Churchill, and his daughter Mary an officer in the ATS, was; General Wavell, who had flown from India for the trip; Brigadier Orde Wingate, the man who had led the 14th Army in Burma; the three Chiefs of Staff; Lord Mountbatten, who was Chief of Combined Operations and 200 others from the UK. Churchill himself was going on to Quebec for a conference known as 'Quadrant'. They arrived in Quebec City on Gibson's twenty-fifth birthday, he was asked by the reporters if Churchill called him by his first name, Gibson replied, 'No, he calls me Dambuster.' On 19 August 1943 he was in Quebec City at No. 8 Air Observation School, the next day Gibson flew from Quebec to Montreal, with him on the flight was Air Vice-Marshal Billy Bishop, who had won the VC in the First World War. On 21 August he flew from Oshawa to Toronto, he did not, as with the previous trip, fly the aircraft; this was left to a Pilot Officer Young.

On 26 August 1943 he held a press conference in Ottawa, then on to Brantford on 1 September, Centralia on 3 September (at a wings parade) and then London on 6 September. His visit took him to New York and Winnipeg, Yorkton, and Moose Jaw and on 8 September to Calgary. It was here that he met the mother of Harlo Taerum, his navigator on the dams operation. He went to her home and spent several hours in her company, what it would have been to have been a fly on the wall in her home. Only days later she received a telegram; 'Regret to advise that your son, Flying Officer Torger Harlo Taerum, DFC, was missing after operations on 15 September 1943.' He had been flying with Wing Commander George Holden, DFC, on an operation to bomb the Dortmund-Emms Canal, an old target for Bomber Command. His aircraft was hit by flak and the Lancaster crashed into a farmhouse in the Hesperweg and the Tallboy bomb blew up, all the crew and the farmer's wife were killed. All but one of the crew that flew with Gibson on the dams raid were killed. Gibson described Harlo as a good pal with a soft Canadian accent. He also said he was probably the most efficient navigator in the squadron.

She sadly lost another son, Lorner Clifford, an air gunner, killed on 3 February 1945 with 550 Squadron. He was, at eighteen, one of the youngest men to be shot down and is buried in Oploo, The Netherlands. It was thought his aircraft, Lancaster PD 221-R, piloted by Flying Officer Robert Nye, age 23, was shot down by a fighter. In Moose Jaw, Gibson met Ken Brown's family and said what a good friend he had in Ken, but did not tell them about the three charges he had been put on by Gibson.

Harlo's mother kept an album which was dark green, in which were many things and gave an insight between herself, her son, Guy Gibson and the dams raid. Harlo had joined the RCAF when Norway was invaded in 1940, although he had never been to Norway his family background was there. When she knew Gibson was coming to visit her she typed out five written lines – things she would say to him.

> I am really thrilled Wing Commander Gibson. I have been looking forward to meeting you.
>
> I feel as though I had known you for some time. Harlo has said so much about you in letters.
>
> How was Harlo when you last saw him?
>
> When you go back to England Wing Commander Gibson, tell Harlo that we are all well at home.
>
> This has been a real privilege, and one I will never forget.

Upon being introduced to Mrs Taerum he said, 'I'm awfully glad to meet you. You are the living image of him you know, or should I say he is the living image of you? Terry is a great boy and a great navigator. He got the whole squadron to the dam.'

Newspapers were full of the meeting, on 11 September the *Calgary Herald* read; 'VC Dam Buster arrives here today' and the following day 'Terry Got Dam Busters to the job Wing Commander Gibson tells his mother here'.

The next day he went to Banff and then returned to Calgary where Mrs Taerum showed him her album and had it autographed. In the album she put the invitation to the investiture that Harlo had sent home to her, also photographs of the men decorated at the palace were put in this album, one wonders where this album is today.

Harlo sent his mother a telegram on 9 May 1943, a week before the dams raid, all it said was 'best wishes'.

While on the tour, Gibson was asked by one lady; 'how many operations have you been over Germany?'

'One hundred and seventy-four.' Not a word was said.

In Calgary, he also met 'Dinghy' Young's brother Robert who was training to be an air gunner, Gibson told him, 'Pilots are not everything, other members of the crew have just as important parts to play.' On 13 September 1943 he moved on to Vancouver and the next day to Montreal, his tour of Canada went to many other towns and cities and then into the USA. On 12 October 1943 he flew to Washington, where he was invested with the Legion of Merit (Commander) by General 'Hap' Arnold of the US Army Air Force. On his return on 1 December, talks were ongoing about a film by the Public Relations Department of the Air Ministry; this received warm approval, but for some reason never went ahead. During his tour he made 150 speeches and broadcasts.

On 1 September 1943, in Brantford, Ontario, Gibson met Premier George Drew, the Premier said it was very pleasant and Gibson, known as Mr Dam-Buster said, 'I was very pleased to meet the Premier.'

The Premier went on to say, 'Here is one of those about whom it was said "Never in the history of mankind has so much been owed by so many to so few." Here is one of the young men who stood between freedom and a German victory. I'm proud to be here.

'It is good for us to have young men like these around. Perhaps heroes are too near to us for their actions to seem real; but history will record the part they played and our children will know how much they meant to us. This congenial young man has played one of the greatest parts to stage our destiny.'

In his speech in return Gibson said, 'A few civilians may have been killed, but you can't help that. Germany started a foul war and we've got to show them we can be as foul and a lot more foul.'

On 3 January 1944, he was posted to the Air Ministry Directorate-Prevention of Accidents, as its Deputy Director, a strange post for a man of such statue and experience. It would appear that not having taken a break from operational flying was his downfall, as he had flown so many operations since 1939 that he had run out of leeway to continue flying. It was while he was at the Air Ministry that he wrote his book *Enemy Coast Ahead*, which one is told, he was told to write. To assist him, Sergeant Jim Heveron was given a two-day pass, Gibson asked him to bring with him the 540/541, the official name for the 617 Squadron operations book, showing all operations and crews operating. This can now be seen in the National Archives. Jim found Gibson in a small room at the Air Ministry in the Kingsway, London. He was very depressed not being able to fly again. While they were together Jim asked if he would write him a reference for a job when the war had ended. Gibson was as good as his word, as it arrived a few days later on Jim's desk at Scampton. It was top-class and helped Jim get a good secure job in 1946. Perhaps he felt that this made up for Jim not getting an award after the dams raid. Also, while at the Air Ministry in February, Gibson was asked to take part in the BBC's *Desert Island Discs* with Roy Plomley, the man who designed the programme. He chose *The Warsaw Concerto*, *Where or When* by the Geraldo orchestra, *A Thousand and One Nights* by Strauss, *The Flying Dutchman* an overture by Wagner, the *Marines March* and the *RAF March Past*, ending with the *Ride of the Valkyries,* again by Wagner. He said, when interviewed over the pieces, that he found choosing them easy as he had often hummed them, his wife Eve also helped him with the choice. *The Warsaw Concerto* was the soundtrack for the film *Dangerous Moonlight* shown in 1941; it also got the name later of *Suicide Squadron*. He said the *Ride of the Valkyries* reminded him of a bombing raid.

(Author – I remember on one occasion visiting the Mohne Dam and playing this piece as we approached the dam and how moving it was, just like a Lancaster running towards the dam.)

There were things in his book that later were found to be untrue, such as his selecting all the crews for the dams raid, he did of course have pilots from 106, his old squadron and he would have also known about men such as Mick Martin, whose illegal low flying was well known in Bomber Command, but there were others who had very little operational experience. One assumes that to have taken all the best crews out of the main air force squadrons and in some ways 'stars' of Bomber Command as a foundation of a new squadron, would have caused a rumpus amongst squadron commanders. This myth was compounded by Brickhill, not only in this instance but in others, probably on the basis of who can doubt Gibson's word; he was after all there at the time. It would have been Jim Heveron as the orderly room sergeant who typed up the battle order for 16 May 1943.

Of the 133 men who had taken off to attack the Ruhr dams, fifty-three were killed, three had been taken prisoner so were not back until the end of the war. Of the remaining seventy-seven survivors a number were not destined to survive the war.

The first to lose their lives was Squadron Leader David Maltby and his crew, flying in Lancaster JA 981 'N' on 14 September 1943 and returning from an aborted trip to the Dortmund-Emms Canal, as he turned to abort, the wingtip hit the sea. The crash was seen by Flight Leader David Shannon, who stayed in the area for over two and half hours until an air-sea rescue launch arrived, sadly only one body was found – David Maltby. His Dambuster crew were never found and have no known grave, but are on the Runneymede Memorial. He is now buried in Wickhambreaux (St Andrew) Churchyard, Kent. Another theory of how he crashed was that in turning, he collided with a Mosquito, DZ598, of 139 Squadron, on route back from Berlin and flown by Flight Lieutenant Maule W. Colledge and his navigator Flying Officer Geoffrey L. Marshall. The crash took place at 0040 hours, eight miles north-east of Cromer, Norfolk. There was an eighth member of Maltby's crew, his name Warrant Officer John L. Walsh, a very experienced air gunner with the DFM, the remainder were the crew that had attacked the Mohne Dam in May. His body was picked up by an air-sea rescue launch of 24 ASR Gorleston. Flight Lieutenant Lance Howard represented 617 Squadron at the funeral. He had flown with Bill Townsend on the dams raid. Maltby's death was well recorded in *The Times*. In a local Kent newspaper he was hailed as 'German Dams Hero Killed'.

Today in private hands exists the wooden bombsight used by Pilot Officer John Fort on the dams raid. At the site of John Hopgood's crash a 12-year-old boy picked up a charred triangular piece of wood, but looking for a souvenir as did most boys in the UK, he threw it away because of its condition, this was the bombsight used by Jim Fraser. It does show that in at least two of the dams aircraft they did use the conventional bombsight.

In St Mary's Church, Sherburn, Co Durham, is a plaque to Flight Sergeant Vivian Nicolson. Sergeant William Hatton is remembered on the memorial board at his old school in Wakefield; Sergeant Anthony Stone had a memorial bench in the grounds of Winchester Cathedral. Harold Simmonds name is in a book of remembrance in

Burgess Hill, Sussex. Sergeant Victor Hill is on a memorial at Berkeley Castle, Gloucestershire, where he had been the head gardener.

Flying with the now Wing Commander George Holden, DFC, who had taken over 617 Squadron from Gibson, was Gibson's crew from the dam raids. On 16 September 1943, twenty miles from the target, Holden's Lancaster was hit in the petrol tank by light flak. It hit the ground at Nordhorn-Altendorf, crashing into a farmhouse. The farmer's wife and all the Lancaster crew were killed; it was Holden's thirtieth birthday. All Gibson's crew, apart from Pulford, whom it appears was still sick, were killed. One of those was Harlo Taerum whose mother Gibson had met only twelve days previously.

   Another pilot who had taken a major part in the dam's raid was also lost on this operation. Les Knight was down as number six to bomb the target on 16 September, as they were about to attack the canal, the bomb aimer, Flying Officer Johnson said, 'High Ground ahead!' Les pulled the column back, but it was too late and they hit the top of the trees, this punctured both radiators and the port engine. As he had difficulty in controlling the engines it was possible the fins and rudder were also damaged. However, he managed to drop his bomb and reached 1,500 feet when the port inner engine started to trail white smoke, the flight engineer, Ray Grayston, feathered it, but as he did the port outer also began to trail white smoke and was also feathered. With both port engines out of action Les had great difficulty in flying on a straight course. The rear turret did not work, owing to the port engine controlling the turret hydraulics, so Sergeant Harry O'Brian came forward to the bomb aimer's area, Les was pushing on the port rudder bar and Harry pulling hard with all his strength. Because of the strain the starboard engines were over-heating, so the port inner engine was restarted, but it again began to smoke.

   Les now realized he would not make the North Sea, so gave the order no pilot wants to do – bale out. Out they went one by one until only Les was left flying the doomed aircraft. He tried to land in a small field with a wire fence across it, but the aircraft crashed, bursting into flames and Les was killed outright.

   So another Dambuster had perished. Bob Kellow, Hobday, Sutherland and Johnson evaded capture and arrived back in the UK. Ray Grayston was taken prisoner and ended up in Stalag III, and Harry O'Brian ended up in L6 POE (No. 519), and then (No. 357) at Kopernikus.

A plaque has now been put up at Den Ham, The Netherlands, at the place Les Knight crashed. On the wooden cross over his grave in 1943 was, Offr L.G. Knight RAAF + 16.9.43 Hier Runt. But later it had Aus F/Lt L.G. Knight, DSO, K/A, 16/9/43.

In 1954 his mother Nellie visited his grave and in the 1980s, Bob Kellow, a former member of his crew.

Post-war, Hobday visited the area and was given his parachute harness, which had been stored away awaiting his return one day.

Sidney Hobday

Flight Lieutenant Harold Wilson and his crew, a reserve for the dams raid were also lost. Having been hit by flak he made a belly landing and blew up, the rear turret, with gunner Sergeant Eric Hornby still inside, was found on the northern side of the Mittelland Canal, with the body of the aircraft on the southern side. The flight engineer was Sergeant Denis Powell who had flown with Bill Townsend on the dams raid; he had been given a mention in despatches on 7 June 1943. Flight Sergeant William Divall and crew, another reserve crew on the dams raid, was also lost on this operation.

On 13 October 1943 the gap to the spillway level at the Eder Dam had been filled. On the Mohne the breach has been filled with concrete to the spillway and the roof of the control towers removed.

On 10 December 1943, Wing Commander Leonard Cheshire was asked to supply four aircraft for S.O.E operations and be attached to 138/161 Squadron at Tempsford. One of the four Lancasters was flown by Flying Officer Gordon Weeden, aged 23, he was lost in France dropping arms to the S.O.E, his aircraft was ED 923-Tommy, which had been flown by Flight Lieutenant Joe McCarthy on the dams raid.

In 2007 the site of the crash was visited by George 'Johnny' Johnson, who was McCarthy's bomb aimer on the dams raid, pieces of the aircraft were excavated. Another dams aircraft lost on this raid was flown by Warrant Officer Bull, ED 886-O had been flown by Flight Sergeant Bill Townsend on the dams raid.

On 16 December 1943, nine aircraft were detailed to attack the construction works at Flixecourt/ Domart-en-Ponthieu, in Northern France.

Another crew who had taken part in the dams raid were lost. Geoff Rice, who was on his way back from the target, not having bombed because of adverse weather conditions, was hit by a night fighter which set the bomber on fire. Geoff gave the order to bale out and then remembered nothing. When baling out he had hit his head and gone unconscious, it was 0830 hours the next day when he woke up with his parachute wrapped around a tree. His crashed aircraft was around him, he had a broken wrist and a severe cut over his left eye. As he managed to walk across the wood he met three farm labourers, who, when he told them he was British took him to a farm. 'Here I was washed, as I was covered in blood, and given civilian clothing. From there we went to another farm where I slept for six hours and then on to a village which I thought was Forchies-la-Marche and spent the night with a café proprietor, his wife and mother. The following day I was taken to Pieton and stayed for five days over Christmas.' They then arranged for a doctor to X-ray and set his wrist in plaster.

He was then taken by a Gendarme to a hospital run by sisters at Morlanwelz. The Gendarme visited him every day and he stayed there for five days. From there he was taken to stay with a dentist at La Louviere. He claimed to be English, but had married a Belgian lady and had lived there for some time. His next move was to another village, Chapelle, and stayed with a French Roman Catholic priest, he said that some of the people there were not too friendly. He was then taken back to La Louviere in a hurry, where he stayed one night; here he was given documents such as an ID card. From there he went to the home of an old lady at Binche where he stayed for several days, but as it was in the centre of town he was moved to an outlying house with two old people. They were killed later when an auxiliary tank from a Mosquito dropped on the their house.

A man said to work for Fairey Aviation Works came and took him to Chareroi and from there by train to Brussels. Here he stayed with an old lady who was blind and looked after him very well.

From there he stayed in a flat with a young couple for ten weeks. He was then moved to the flat of a hospital d'Ixcelles, with him there was a US Lieutenant bomb aimer, Charles Betzel. From there they caught a train to Antwerp. Two men picked them up near the station and gave them a meal, one of them then left to find accommodation, but came back with the secret police. Rice had been free for five months. He spent the rest of the war at Stalag III and Stalag IIIA. He was liberated at Luckenwalde by Russian forces on 21 April 1945.

The rest of his Dambuster crew were killed in the crash. Later it was reported that Sergeant Chester Gowrie, RCAF, the wireless operator, had survived the crash but been shot by the Germans.

On 12 February 1944, an attack on the Antheor Viaduct was carried out by ten 617 Squadron Lancasters. In the target area, Mick Martin was subject to heavy anti-aircraft fire from a 20mm cannon on the viaduct itself and bomb aimer Bob Hay, who had been the bombing leader on the dams raid was killed and Ivan Whittaker the flight

Flight Lieutenant Bob Hay's grave in Sardinia. © Corporal Crowe RAF

engineer wounded in the legs. Mick flew the Lancaster to Sardinia, which was now occupied by the Americans, Bob Hay was buried here and Whittaker put into hospital. So another Dambuster had died.

Bob Hay became one of many men from the Commonwealth who became a victim of war and one of 56,000 men killed in Bomber Command in the Second World War. He now rests in peace in St Michael's Cemetery, Caliari, many miles from his homeland of Australia.

Let us not forget the efforts and courage of Bob Hay and the many other men from the Commonwealth who came in our desperate hour of need. Within two days of war being declared the Commonwealth countries had also declared themselves as being at war with Germany. The old country needed them and they were coming to help.

However, the losses did not end there. The remaining Lancasters landed and stayed the night at RAF Ford, now a prison. Flying with Squadron Leader Bill Suggitt was Gibson's flight engineer Sergeant John Pulford and they took off to fly back to RAF Woodhall Spa, but as they came down through low cloud the Lancaster hit the ground at Littleton Down, which at 836 feet above sea-level was the highest point in the South Downs of Sussex. All the crew, apart from Suggitt who died two days later,were killed outright. Pulford was buried in Hull, his home town.

In the parish church of the village near the crash site of Upwaltham, West Sussex, a memorial to KC J-Jug DV 382 was unveiled in 2009. The memorial, called the Four Nations Memorial, is at the church of St Mary the Virgin and has the names of all the crew of DV 382, including of course John Pulford.

On 30 March 1944, came the infamous Nuremburg raid in which ninety-six bombers failed to return. Flying in the rear turret of a 97 Pathfinder Squadron Lancaster was Flight Lieutenant Richard Trevor-Roper, DFC, DFM, who had flown with Guy Gibson on the dams raid, today he is buried in the Durnbach War Cemetery, near Munich.

Sergeant Brian Jagger, who had flown with David Shannon as front gunner was killed on 30 April 1944, when flying in a Lancaster of 49 Squadron on a fighter affiliation exercise. The dinghy became released and wrapped itself around the tailplane. He is now buried in Cambridge City Cemetery.

The last man to lose his life, who had taken part in the dams raid, was the leader, Wing Commander Guy Gibson, VC, DSO, DFC. After the dams raid he had been taken off flying, something he never got over, but on 19 September 1944, when based at RAF Coningsby, he flew a Mk XX Mosquito, KB 267, on a raid to Rheydt as a Pathfinder Master Bomber. A force of 236 Lancasters and ten Mosquitos was despatched to attack two important railway lines, one from Aachen and the other Cologne. These railway lines met at Rheydt, before running on to Monchengladbach two miles away, then connecting with the main route from the Ruhr to Venlo and Holland. With large railway yards, capable of handling 2,500 waggons every twenty-four hours, and several important engineering works, it was a target of great importance and heavily defended by flak and fighters.

For some reason the bomber plot was not passed to the German chain of command until 2143 hours, when the bombers were actually on approach to the target. The Mosquito he was supposed to use was unserviceable, so he went over to Woodhall Spa and 627 Squadron, where the Commanding Officer, Wing Commander Curry, DSO, DFC, authorized him to use KB 267-E. The Mosquito he used for the operation was, according to Peter Mallender who normally used it, the best on the squadron.

On the day, having been asked to brief them on the details of the aircraft, he took Gibson and Squadron Leader James Warwick, his navigator, out to the Mosquito; upon which Gibson told him that as they had flown the Mosquito before he did not need a briefing. KB 267 was a Canadian model and the fuel cocks were behind the pilot and not in the cockpit below the pilot's area, so besides the fact that Warwick had not flown in a Mosquito before, it was Peter's view that the reason they crashed was that Warwick, Gibson's navigator, could not find them in time and the engines cut out. Gibson himself had only eleven hours on the Mosquito, probably the English version with the fuel cocks in the area of the pilot and not as in KB 267, behind him.

Gibson had been due to have Pilot Officer Dai Thomas as his navigator, but he went down with flu, which as it is saved his life, his place was taken by Squadron Leader Jim Warwick who had just been awarded a DFC after twenty-five operations with 49 Squadron. One operation in his tour was the raid on Peenemunde, led by Group Captain John Searby, who had been a Flight Commander under Gibson at 106 Squadron in 1942/43. Jim came from Belfast and had joined up in September 1941.

A number of men of 101 Squadron remember hearing Gibson on the air and at the second aiming point Gibson had a hang up on his Target Indicators.

The last contact with Gibson was when he came on the air and said, 'Okay, that's fine, now home.' Some while later he was seen with flames coming from the aircraft over Steenbergen and it crashed in a field of a farm owned by Mr van der Riet. The Germans sealed off the area within thirty minutes. Eye witnesses had heard his engine splutter before crashing. Many theories have been put forward – as with the loss of Major Glen Miller – such as running out of fuel, the changing over of fuel tanks which would have been done by Warwick, and being shot down by a rear gunner in one of the Lancasters of 61 Squadron, thinking the Mosquito was a German fighter, also that flying low he had been hit by a bomber dropping its bombs from above. But Squadron Leader Rupert Oakley, who later commanded 627 Squadron, thought he had too few hours on the Mosquito, at most Gibson had eleven hours. It would also appear that the Mosquito was often mistaken for a JU88.

Mosquito AZ-E KB 267 was a built in Toronto, one of 1,134 Mosquitos built in Canada, and one of 245 Mk XX's built. It had the dark upper body with black undersides, wings, fuselage and the Pathfinder white stripes on the wings and fuselage. One such Mosquito with ED 267 marks can be seen at RAF Cosford.

In 1985 the wreckage of Gibson's Mosquito was dug up by the Netherlands Air Force salvage team. In Steenbergen a street has been named after Gibson and one after Warwick.

As Rupert Oakley explained, changing over the petrol cocks so as not to starve the engines of fuel was a critical time. It could give the impression the aircraft was on fire – because of the white flames coming from the exhaust pipes – if one is too slow in changing from the main empty tank to a full one.

Another possibility was that when flying low, if you pushed forward on the stick to hug the contours of the land the engine would cut out with the negative 'G' and then, after a second or so, would recover. At night, this recovery was accompanied by quite a glare from the exhausts. Again this may be what the eye witness saw. If Gibson had been close to stall and pushed forward on the stick to gain speed, it would have been fatal at low altitude.

It was only when Steenbergen was liberated that the true identification was made and two wooden crosses put up. Today the now well-known war graves headstones have been put up at the Steenbergen Kruisland Roman Catholic Churchyard.

Peter Mallender went to Steenbergen after the war and while there he made a point of making enquiries about the crash. He was told that none of the Dutch had seen any other aircraft nearby, or heard any gunfire, just a low flying British intruder aircraft. He was also told that a light had been seen moving around the cockpit; this, Peter surmised, was Warwick using a torch to try and find the fuel cocks which were behind the pilot. In Peter's opinion, this was the loss of a great pilot and RAF colleague, whose arrogance in not accepting his advice at Woodhall Spa prior to taking off, led to his death. Also the fact he had not taken the Mosquito Pathfinder course at Warboys and the provision that Air Vice-Marshal Cochrane had given him when he requested to fly on operations. If Cochrane had known, he would have withdrawn permission for him to fly on 19 September 1944. In the opinion of Group Captain Hamish Mahaddie, the recruiting officer for the Pathfinder Force, it would have benefitted him greatly.

Back in the UK, when Gibson was posted as missing, a security clamp was put into operation. If he had baled out and was on the

The site of Guy Gibson's crash, Steenbergen

run in Europe, they did not want the Germans to be alerted, with his reputation after the dams raid it was obvious that capturing Gibson would have been of great delight to the Germans. But it would appear it got out, as a lorry driver who gave a lift to a 627 Squadron navigator said, 'That was tough luck on Guy Gibson last night'.

Mrs Eve Gibson was sent a letter from Winston Churchill expressing his sadness at the news of her husband's death. It is said he may well have been recommended a bar to his VC, but nothing came of it. She and Guy had just set up home in London at Aberdeen Place, off the Edgware Road. Today there is a blue plaque outside the house they had lived in. There is also a blue plaque outside a house in Archer Road, Penarth, South Wales, where he also lived and the family home of his wife Eve.

The Deputy Mayor of Steenbergen reported:

> At 2330 hours, in the territory of the municipality in the Westgraff hendrik polder, about one and half miles from the centre of the municipality, a British aircraft 'Merlin KB 267, Lockheed 22, Mark 3,3 crashed in flames.' The crew were thrown out by the explosion.

> Found at the scene of the crash;
> One silver ring, gold plated with the initials J.B.W.
> ID plate with J.B. Warwick Offr Press 156612 RAFVR
> A damaged wristwatch mark 'Omega'
> Two clasps
> One black tie
> An envelope with the address, S/Ldr J.B. Warwick, DFC.

> Also,
> One sock with 'Gibson' marked on it
> French, and Belgium currency, maps, stamps and a forage cap.

All these items were sent to the Netherlands Red Cross.

As there was a curfew at 2000 hours in Steenbergen, not many people saw the crash. They wanted a ceremonial funeral but the German commander ordered the bodies to be buried within the hour. They were buried by a Mr Sloven, a resident in Steenbergen. It was only when Steenbergen was liberated and the bodies correctly identified, that two wooden crosses were put up over the graves to their memory. It is also interesting that Gibson was recorded as being with 627 Squadron at the time of his death, when of course he was only using a 627 Squadron aircraft, both he and Warwick were actually on the personnel of 54 Base, Coningsby.

In 2010, the Municipality of Steenbergen opened its Dambuster Trail, the 2.9 kilometre walk leads to the Gibson and Warwick graves in the Roman Catholic Cemetery, and on to the Hotel Aarden, where there is a mini exhibition and then on to the crash site in what was the Westgraaf Hendrikpolder.

In the *Congleton Courier* the headlines were; 'Wing Commander Gibson VC missing.' If he had lived he may well have become an MP for Macclesfield.

If you look at his lack of flying for over eighteen months, failing to take the Pathfinder Course was a contributory factor in failing to return and the end of a magnificent career as an officer and airmen.

On 23 September 1943 another casualty from the dams raid was Pilot Officer Cyril Anderson. He had returned to 49 Squadron after the raid, but was shot down and killed on a raid to Mannheim. Previous to this he had flown on operations to Wuppertal, Cologne – twice, Hamburg – twice, Turin, Essen etc. all heavily defended targets. This was his twenty-third operation and 136 hours flying.

His aircraft was seen to come down out of the sky in a fireball and crashed between Offenbach and Isheim. Ernst Fuchs, who was twelve at the time, went to the area of the crash and found men lying dead all over the fields. The sight he saw that day remained with him all his life. The Lancaster, ED 702-D-Donald, was delivered to 49 Squadron in March 1943, about the time that Cyril and his crew joined the squadron. It had been regarded as the Squadron Commander, Wing Commander Slee's personal aircraft, as commanding officer he would not fly on every operation and on occasions such as this, others would use the aircraft.

There were reports that the area of Mannheim was heavily defended with fighters on 23 September 1943 and it was first thought he was shot down by Oberleutnant Lenz Finster from 2/NJG1. He was buried in the local church by the residents and the service held by the Roman Catholic priest Revd. Jakob Storck. The information proved to be incorrect. The aircraft had crashed near Landau and that they had been shot down by Leutnant Heinz Grimm, a holder of the Knight's Cross.

Pilot Officer Cyril Anderson's grave.
© *Alan Cooper*

Revd. Storck reported that a bomber had come down near the church of Insheim, he went on to say all the crew were killed and that two had tried to bale out but were killed. Five of the crew were buried on 26 September and two on 28 September. It is possible that the two reported as trying to bale out had been thrown from the aircraft when it exploded. In 1948, Cyril Anderson and his crew were exhumed and buried in the Commonwealth War Graves Cemetery in Rheinberg. The body of Cyril was identified by a signet ring and a chromium cigarette case with an unusual Tiger design on it. The area of their burial in the churchyard was never used again.

Other information that has come in over the years is that Leutnant Heinz Grimm had attacked the Lancaster using the Schrage Musik method of attack, when they came up under the bomber and hit the fuel tanks, setting the aircraft on fire. It then exploded over Insheim, and crashed into a field. Dominic Howard, the nephew of Cyril

Anderson, after looking at all the statements, deduced that having been hit by Grimm's attack they tried to force-land, but as they looked for an area to bring the Lancaster down it exploded and came down in two parts. The front part, it is believed, came down in a maize crop. He has been back a few times and found the area of the crash and with excavation found a number of pieces of aircraft and sadly an RAF button. His plan was to go back in 2012 and try to locate the front part of the Lancaster.

Father Storck retired to Weselberg and died there in 1960, aged 75.

Along with Cyril, who was 29, was; Robert Patterson from Edinburgh, he like Cyril had joined the RAF as ground crew in 1938, he was 34; John Nugent, from Stormy Middleton, Derby, aged 29, he had been a teacher prior to the war; William Bickle from Knotty Ash, Liverpool; Gilbert Green, aged 21, from Southall, Middlesex; Eric Ewan, age 21, from Wolverhampton and Arthur Buck, aged 28, from Beckenham, Kent. They flew together, died together and now lay in peace together. A tree has been planted at East Kirkby in memory of Cyril and his gallant crew.

Cyril was described as a quiet man and a true gentleman. Wherever he was posted to, Rose his wife would try and be housed near and he used a motorbike to get him back and forth. Rose always said that if he had stayed as ground crew he would have survived the war. But he always wanted to fly. She died in 1999 and Cyril's name was inscribed on her headstone, also baby Graham, who had also died in 1943.

Post-war his family have visited his grave in the Rheinberg War Cemetery and taken soil from the UK to put on his grave and soil from his grave had been taken back to plant in the UK.

From December 1942, monthly reports on losses and interception of Bomber Command aircraft on night operations had drawn attention to the following:

- A high proportion of attacks made on bombers from below.
- A high proportion of attacking fighters not being seen.
- A high proportion of damage resulting from such attacks.
- Bombers being hit without warning from cannon shells from below and not having seen a fighter.
- The Germans used an ME 110 aircraft equipped with the Schrage Musik upwards-firing cannon.

The pilots who operated the gun would aim to hit the bomber between the two nacelles on either side, or if the rear gunner was alerted, the fire would be focused on him. This was introduced because the Ju88 and ME 110 had difficulty matching the speeds of the Lancaster and the Halifax – when approached from astern and below – for an attack with normal firing guns. By the time January 1944 came 3.2 per cent were deemed to have been destroyed by the upward-firing gun and in April it reached a peak of 13.3 per cent.

Between August and December 1946 the thirty-seven Upkeep bombs were flown out to sea and dropped in the Atlantic, some 280 miles west of Glasgow. The Lancasters used for this were brought out of storage and three original Dambuster aircraft; ED 906 flown on the raid by Maltby and later scrapped on 29 July 1947; ED 909, Mick Martin's aircraft, also scrapped on the same day and ED 932, Guy Gibson's Lancaster on the dams raid, this was also scrapped in July 1947. All bombs or mines were dropped from 10,000 feet.

CHAPTER 12

Post-War

In December 1946, McGowan Cradon offered his services as 617 Squadron's historian. He was an intelligence officer and had been recommended for this post by Group Captain Leonard Cheshire, VC, and a former commanding officer of 617 Squadron. He himself had been asked to take on the task of writing the history of 617 Squadron and had consented, but then other work and health forced him to drop the idea. Cradon however, was rejected on the grounds he had spent too much time with 617 Squadron aircrew and got in many practice flights with them, when he should have been attending to his job as an intelligence officer, this was frowned upon by the powers that be and the reason his offer was turned down.

In 1949, the head of the Air Historical Branch, John Nerney, was approached by John Pudney, who was involved with BBC Television. He suggested that a book on 617 Squadron should be written by Paul Brickhill, an Australian writer who himself had been a pilot and a prisoner of war. He had written a book with Conrad Norton called *Escape to Danger*, which was then being made into a TV series. The end result was a book written by Brickhill in 1950 called *The Dam Busters*.

Much has been made of this book over the years, although I did see a letter some years ago that had been sent to Brickhill, it questioned what he had written about later 617 Squadron operations. The reply from Brickhill said that what he could not find out, 'he had made up'.

On 16 December 1949, Barnes Wallis wrote to Sir Archibald Rowlands, KCB, MBE, the personal secretary of Vickers Armstrong Limited. He said in his letter that he had been given permission to make a personal application for an award for the invention that brought about the destruction of the Mohne and Eder Dams. He again

Mohne Dam today. © Alan Cooper

wrote on 20 December and said it was his intention to ask for such an award.

Both Upkeep and Highball were on the 'Top Secret' list, as was the technical information, films and official reports relating to them. He also believed that the Ministry of Supply held information and reports on the bombs that had been found in Germany. He then asked for permission, and the authority, to ask for such material as he found necessary in preparing his statement of claim to be made available.

On 1 March 1950, Barnes Wallis submitted his statement to the Royal Commission on Awards to Inventors. It gave his full name of Barnes Neville Wallis; address White Hill House, Effingham, Surrey. His position as, Chief of Aeronautical Research and Development, Aviation Section Vickers. His service in the armed forces or government department is also of interest: Corporal Artists Rifles 1915; Sub-Lt R.N.V.R (Air) 1915; Sergeant R.A. A-A Battery T.D. 1922–1925.

He ended his statement by saying that he had collaborated with Wing Commander Gibson in evolving a scheme for training his squadron in the particular technique required by an attack with this weapon, and that he was actually responsible for briefing him and his crews immediately before the raid.

On 8 March 1951 the question of awards in the Birthday Honours of 1943 was raised.

Also on that day, Air Marshal Sir R. Victor Goddard, KCB, CBE, wrote to Air Chief Marshal Sir Leslie N. Hollinghurst, KCB, KBE, DFC, concerning the scholarship for sons of RAF Officers at Christ's Hospital (Bluecoat School). It said that Barnes Wallis of Vickers, expected to receive a War Inventions award for his Mohne Dam bomb. This was likely to be in the region of £20,000 or more, and that he was going to give the whole amount to Christ's Hospital fund, being the Governor and an Old Blue.

Goddard had written to Wallis and asked him to persuade his colleagues on the board of the School to make some variations to the rules of admission. No boy was allowed to go to Christ's Hospital unless the income of his parents was less than, 'I think,' as he went on to say, '£800 a year'. This would rule out the children of senior officers. However, Goddard believed they deserved special consideration as they could not send their children to ordinary day schools owing to constant changes of home, and postings. Obviously Wallis thought this was worthy of consideration.

The letter also said that the award of the CBE to Mr Wallis was made in recognition of his work in connection with geodetic construction used in the airframes of the Wellesley and Wellington bombers.

After careful consideration and a long delay, on 15 March 1951, the Royal Commission for inventions recommended that an ex gratia payment of £10,000 be made to Mr B.N.Wallis, for inventive contribution relating to bombs. He donated the whole amount to Christ's Hospital School, who set up an RAF foundations trust to allow children of RAF personnel killed or injured in action to attend the school. Such was his grief over the losses on the dams raid.

The making of the film started in 1953 and it became a classic British black and white film with a cast of people, some already established, but others who went on to become established stars of the British screen. The premier for the film was done over two days 16 and 17 May 1955, at the Empire Theatre, Leicester Square. On 16 May 1955, fourteen of the original members of 617 Squadron were introduced to Princess Margaret.

They were: R. E. Grayston; H.S. Hobday, DFC; E.C. Johnson, DFC; W.C. Townsend, CGM, DFM; D.E. Webb, DFM; H.B. Martin, DSO, DFC; I. Whittaker, DFC; B.T. Foxlee, DFM; B. Goodale, DFC; J. Buckley, DFC; E.E. Appleby; W. Howarth, DFM; G. Rice, DFC and H. J. Hewstone.

And 17 May they were: J.C. McCarthy, DSO, DFC; D.R. Walker, DFC; D.A. McLean, DFC; K.A. Brown, CGM; P.E. Pigeon, DFC; R. Wilkinson, DFM; F. Tees; H.B. Feneron; D.P. Heal, DFM; A.F. Burcher, DFM; L.J. Sumpter, DFC, DFM and C.E. Franklin, DFM.

On 17 May 1955, they were introduced to the Duke and Duchess of Gloucester. On 16 May, Eve Hyman, formerly Gibson, attended the premier. After the war she had married again, to Jack Hyman, a South African who was later killed in a car accident, in her later life she went back to being Mrs Gibson. With her was Guy's father Alexander, on his seventy-eighth birthday. At the premier he said how Guy had been sorry about the animals killed when the dam had burst. Among those present on 17 May were Tony Burcher – who had retired from the RAAF and re-enlisted in the RAF and had been pulled out of the Malayan jungle where he was testing aircrew survival, and for this carried a 50lb pack on his back – and Freddie Tees, both having been prisoners of war after the dams raid, Tony had broken his back and Freddie was badly burnt.

Tony Burcher was brought out of the jungle in Borneo where he was serving with 205 Squadron. He had been promoted to Flight Lieutenant in the RAAF in 1944, but transferred to the RAF in 1952 and served in Korea and Malaya.

On 16 May 1955 it poured with rain as guests turned up for the premier. There was a reception afterwards at the Criterion in Regent Street, where a 9×3 foot model of the Mohne Dam was on display.

On 14 May, prior to the premier, a reception was given at the Louis XV room at the Criterion Restaurant, London, for 617 Squadron, by the RAF Association, British Picture, and the Pathfinder Association. Present was Gibson's father, Bill Kerr, Mick Martin, Joe McCarthy and many others.

The film was based on Paul Brickhill's book *The Dam Busters*, published in 1951 and Guy Gibson's own book *Enemy Coast Ahead*, which was published in 1946. Also present was John Pulford's brother, Mr S. Pulford and Mr J. Whillis, brother of the late Pilot Officer Whillis, who had been in Barlow's crew and Mr A. Yeo, father of Sergeant Yeo of Young's crew.

The film was made by Associated British Pictures Corporation. The Director was Michael Anderson and starred:

Richard Todd, died 2009, age 90,	as Guy Gibson.
Michael Redgrave, knighted in 1959 and died in 1985, age 77,	as Barnes Wallis.
Basil Sydney, died 1968, aged 73,	as Air Chief Marshal Sir Arthur Harris.
Patrick Barr, died 1985, aged 77,	as Captain Mutt Summers.
Ernest Clark, died 1994, aged 82,	as Air Vice-Marshal Hon. Ralph Cochrane.
Derek Farr, died 1986, aged 74,	as Group Captain Whitworth.
Brewster Mason, died 1987, aged 84	as Flight Lieutenant Trevor-Roper, in Gibson's crew.
Tony Doonan,	as Flight Lieutenant Hutchison, in Gibson's crew.
Nigel Stock, died 1986, aged 66,	as Flying Officer Spafford, in Gibson's crew.
Brian Nissen, died 2001, aged 73,	as Flight Lieutenant Taerum, in Gibson's crew.
Peter Assinder, died 2008, aged 85,	as Pilot Officer Deering, in Gibson's crew.
Richard Leech, died 2004, aged 81,	as Squadron Leader Young.
Richard Thorp, died 2013, aged 81,	as Squadron Leader Maudslay.
John Fraser, now 82,	as Flight Lieutenant Hopgood.
David Morrell,	as Flight Lieutenant Astell.
Bill Kerr,	as Flight Lieutenant Martin.
George Baker,	as Flight Lieutenant Maltby.
Ronald Wilson, now 83,	as Flight Lieutenant Shannon.
Denys Graham,	as Flying Officer Knight.
Basil Appleby, now 93,	as Flight Lieutenant Hay.
Tim Turner, died 1987, aged 62,	as Flight Lieutenant Leggo.
Ewen Solon, died 1985, aged 67,	as Flight Sergeant George Powell.
Robert Shaw	as Flight Sergeant John Pulford.

Movie poster for the 1955 epic, The Dam Busters, *directed by Michael Anderson*

Dam Busters *reception party; Wing Commander P.E. Pigeon RCAF (far left) Wing Commander Dunn, the film's director Michael Anderson and Flying Officer Goodale*

Left to right; Charles and Mrs Molly Franklin, Richard Todd. © *Mrs Franklin*

Barnes Wallis, left, with the man who played him in the film, Michael Redgrave

George Baker became famous for *Inspector Wexford*. Sadly, George died in October 2011, aged 80. Robert Shaw also became a very well-known actor, playing in films *From Russia with Love*, *Jaws*, and the *Battle of the Bulge*.

Bill Kerr lives in Australia and became a well-known actor, he is ninety-one. He said of the film: 'It took me two hours of makeup, a wig and a moustache before I really looked like Micky Martin.' He went on to say, 'You know the attention to detail in this Lancaster is incredible – they have done a marvellous job restoring her, and the attention to detail in the original film was extraordinary, they even put chocks in my ears so they stood out to look just like Micky Martin's.' He got the job straight off the boat from Australia and he was driven to Pinewood Studios. He had been in the well-known film *Appointment in London* also a film about Bomber Command released in 1952 and starring Dirk Bogarde. It was written by John Woolridge, who had served as a flight commander in 106 Squadron, then commanded by Guy Gibson, and for some, Bogarde's part was based on Gibson. Amazingly, he also wrote the music for the film. Bill ended by saying it was an honour to play an Australian Dambuster.

Peter Arne was in many well-known films including *The Cockleshell Heroes, Ice Cold in Alex*, and played the Staff Officer to Harris. During the war he had been a pilot in the RAF and later the Fleet Air Arm. When he was killed in 1983, age 62, he was working on what would have been a very interesting autobiography and was to be the next Dr Who.

Gerald Harper played a 57 Squadron RAF Officer, this was his first film, but later went on to make a successful career on TV, in such as *Hadleigh*. He is eighty-three.

Another who later became famous in the UK and the USA, was Patrick McGoohan, he was an RAF Policeman on the door of the briefing room for the dams raid and turned Guy Gibson's dog away. He was later to star in films such as, *The Prisoner, Danger Man* and *Ice Station Zebra*. He died in 2009, aged 80.

Richard Thorp played Maudslay and went on to be Dr John Rennie in *Emergency Ward Ten, Crossroads* and then Alan Turner in *Emmerdale*. He said of his time in the film, 'I loved filming *Dam Busters*. I was very proud to be in it. It made me see how incredibly brave these young men were. The Lancaster bombers used to shake like jellies. I've been up in one and they are freezing cold with the wind rushing right through them.' He died in 2013, aged 81.

The film was released on 24 May 1955 and at the UK box office made £419,528. It had cost £250,000 to make. But of course, as well as in the UK, the film was a big hit in the USA.

The music for the score was composed by Leighton Lucas, a composer and conductor who also wrote the music for *Ice Cold in Alex*. Eric Coates had been approached to compose the whole score, but was advised by no less than Sir Edward

Eric Coates

Elgar not to get into writing film scores. But he did offer a piece he had written a few days previously, this was accepted as the title march and is now one of the most famous war themes ever.

Between 1954 and 1956 over 250,000 copies of the recording were sold, it has been used as a tune for the hymn *'God is our Strength and Refuge'*.

Eric Coates was known as the uncrowned king of music and wrote many famous pieces such as *Calling All Workers*, for *Music While you Work*, the *Sleepy Lagoon*, used later for *Desert Island Discs*, its actual name was *By the Sleepy Lagoon*. Another was the *Knightsbridge March*, later used in the radio programme *In Town Tonight*. He died of a heart attack in the Royal West Sussex Hospital on 21 December 1957.

The majority of the ground filming took place at RAF Hemswell, a few miles from RAF Scampton. Four Lancasters were brought out of storage and flown by pilots of 109 and 139 Squadrons who were based at Hemswell. Three of them had been used for filming in 1952

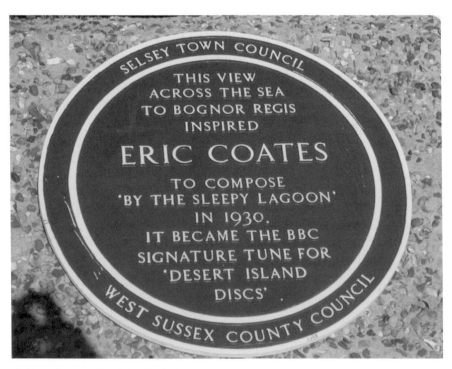

A blue plaque affixed in Coates' memory

for the film *Appointment in London* starring Dirk Bogarde. One of the Lancasters, NX 679, had been on 617 Squadron strength in July 1945. This one had been changed to ED 932-AJ-G, Gibson's Lancaster for the film. NX 673 had been with 9 Squadron in India in 1945, having gone there for the invasion of Japan. All were melted down for scrap in 1956. The cost of the various conversions to a Dambuster type aircraft cost £3,000. NX 673 was used as Hopgood's aircraft and not changed for the film to ED 925-M. The cost was £130 pounds an hour and consumed 10 per cent of the film's budget.

Because the bomb was still on the secret list until 1959 it could not be shown, so something that was thought to be similar to a bouncing bomb was made, security was strict in this area and the mock-up bomb had to be inspected before filming began.

A Wellington T.10 MF 628 was used for the early test runs of the bouncing bomb and now resides in the RAF Museum at RAF Hendon. This is the only Wellington known to have survived, quite remarkable when you think of the number built. Instead of Reculver, where the actual tests were made, Skegness, being nearer Scampton, was used in the film.

The one bit of luck was that, although 5 Group HQ had been turned into flats after the war, in the basement, the 5 Group Operation room was found exactly as it had been left in 1945, completely untouched. It was here that Wing Commander Wally Dunn, OBE, was called in to dub the Morse signals onto the film soundtrack. He was the technical advisor for the film and was invited in 1954, by Michael Anderson, to watch the reconstruction of the attack on the Mohne Dam. Three huge sheds called stages had been set up and part of the floor had been removed, disclosing a sheet of water in the shape of the Mohne Lake, 150 feet wide, 300 feet long and lined with grass and imitation fir trees. In the middle was a model of the dam, it was just like the one Wally had seen eleven years before at Grantham. Alongside the set was a two foot track on which a high speed camera trolley had been mounted, with a cine camera and an aircraft type seat behind it, both placed on a long steel trellis with a swivelling arm. This trolley raced down the track with the camera shooting a side view of the approach to the dam, as it came level with it, a high column of water rose into the air to give the impression of a bomb exploding. Washing powder was added to the water to create foam.

For the film, Wally was put into a soundproof cabinet and could see the film action taking place in the operations room at Grantham. He watched himself on the dais in the ops room and at the appropriate moment transmitted the Morse code – on a service Morse key and valve oscillator – actually dubbing the film with the Morse of each aircraft. A similar sequence was undertaken for the attack on the Eder Dam film.

Wally's son was awarded a British Empire Medal as a Sergeant and went on to be Air Chief Marshal Sir Eric Dunn.

The dog used to portray 'Nigger' was an army mine-detector dog, he played the part perfectly, but would not go anywhere near the real 'Nigger's' grave at RAF Scampton. Richard Todd lived in a hotel in Lincoln while making the film and the dog lived with him. He also described getting the part as 'God's Gift of a Role'. All the main actors were ex-servicemen and found it easy to play the part of Army or RAF officer's/nco's and any re-make of the film would have difficulty in finding actors to play these roles. The film was a great success and even today is a classic.

The script was written by playwright Robert Cedric Sherriff. He had an anti-romantic style and stuck to the film as Michael Anderson required it be written – as a documentary. This was the reason for it being made in black and white monochrome throughout.

One piece of luck – but not for the people there – was that at the period of shooting the film, the Ruhr had heavy flooding.

On 25 May 1955, Sir Winston Churchill wrote to the Rt Hon. Sir Norman Brook, GCB, saying he had seen a very good film called *The Dam Busters* the other night, and in this it was said that he had expressed strong personal support for the operation and had given directions upon the subject. He said he remembered it quite well and that he would be much obliged if Sir Norman could kindly let him have any material, or any record of the decision, which he had made that the attempt should be carried out in May, and also any other material on the subject.

On 7 June 1955, Churchill again wrote to Sir Norman, he said he was sure he had heard about the dams operation in January 1943, before all the lengthy preparations that were made were allowed to begin, and this is the sequence of the story as it appears in *The Dam Busters*.

He said he had authorized his influence to be used to the full. He then asked if it would be possible to inquire from the author of the book, who had great help from the Air Service, on what they based their reference? The part of Paul Brickhill's book that interested Churchill was that it was said in February 1943, 'Churchill and Merton were enthusiastic about it'. This, according to Churchill's own recollections. He wondered whether the author of the book could recall on what statement this was based.

Paul Brickhill, now living in Italy, was approached about this and replied on 20 July 1955. In his reply he said he had not been able to see Merton or Portal during his research and did not approach Churchill as he felt he had enough people on his back at the time. He went on to say that Dr Barnes Wallis understood that Sir Winston had given his approval and that Sir Ralph Cochrane – the wartime leader of 5 Group which 617 Squadron came under – and Captain 'Mutt' Summers the test pilot, confirmed this. He also said that he did not think it could have gone ahead without the approval from Churchill. He ended by saying that Lord Portal was the man to speak to.

On 12 August 1955, Portal was written to on this subject and explained that he was positive that Churchill knew about the dams operation in January 1943, months before it took place. But, he said, his memory of Upkeep was rusty and seemed to think the film exaggerated the technical difficulties involved and he did not remember having to involve the PM, if he had, he said he would have remembered doing so and regretted he could not be of more help.

It is certainly true that after Harris had seen the film of the trials for the dams operation at Chesil beach in February 1943, the papers for Upkeep were sent to Churchill and he gave the green light to go ahead.

In 1958 the Sorpe Dam was drained for bomb damage repairs, during which an unexploded Tallboy bomb was discovered. On 6 January 1959, the inhabitants of the village of Langscheid were evacuated while Westphalia's chief bomb disposal officer, Walter Mietzke , and a British Army Lieutenant, James Waters, defused the 3.6m bomb that still contained 2.5 metric tonnes of high explosive and a highly unstable acid fuse.

In 1962, the dam was repaired using 4,350 tons of cement and 1,700 tons of clay.

The Sorpe Dam. © Horst Muller

On 19 May 1968, to mark the 25th Anniversary of the dams raid, a service was held at St Clement Dane's, the Royal Air Force Church in the Strand. This was preceded on 18 May by a reception and showing of the film at the Warner Theatre, Leicester Square, by Warner Pathe and British Picture Corporation. This was followed by a cocktail party attended by many of the dam's survivors, also Barnes Wallis, Richard Todd, Sir Arthur Harris, Sir Ralph Cochrane, and the former Station Commander, Charles Whitworth. One of the lessons was read by Mick Martin.

In 1972, a reunion was held in Canada over a week, ending with a party to end all parties, in Toronto. About forty Canadian ex-members of 617 Squadron attended, including Ken Brown, Danny Walker, Don McLean and Dave Rodger.

In 1975, a small version of the bouncing bomb was recovered at Reculver by an American Sikorsky helicopter; it would have been dropped by a Wellington or Mosquito. It was on display in Amsterdam until 1995, when it was put into storage at the Dutch Military Aviation Museum. It was then brought back to the UK and is on loan from the RAFA Amsterdam at the RAF Scampton Museum.

In 1976, a reunion was held in Holland, and on 19 May a visit to Gibson's grave, where wreaths were laid by Eve Gibson, and by Miss Ellen Warwick, James Warwick's sister from Belfast.

In 1977, a Vulcan bomber flew over the home of Sir Barnes Wallis in Effingham, Surrey. A white sheet and yellow towel were put in the garden at Beech Lane to guide the aircraft over their house, the occasion was Wallis's ninetieth birthday. Later in the day, at a party in Thatcher's Restaurant in East Horsley, the *Dambuster March* was played and a telegram from the Queen read out. For the party there was a Wellington Cocktail with kiwi and paw-paw fruit, Tornados Barnes Wallis and Airship Meringue.

During the 1977 celebrations, John F. Grime, DFC, recalled an incident. He had just been posted to 207 Squadron at RAF Langer on 16 May 1943. The squadron were on a stand down, but being a new boy he and his crew were down for high-level bombing practice during the morning and a Bullseye exercise that night – the night of the dams raid. It turned out that this was part of the diversion for the raid, but it was the next day before they saw the photographs of the breach and they realized the part they had played in the dams operation.

(Author – In 1978, I spent two days with Sir Barnes Wallis at his home at White Hill House, Effingham, a house that he had built in the 1930s. It backed on to the Effingham golf course. During my time with him upstairs in his study I soon realized that although he was in his nineties, his mind was still as sharp as a needle. While with him I took two photographs of the great man and I think, according to his family, captured – against his full head of white hair – his very blue eyes. Sadly, these turned out to be the last photographs taken of him. When I left him at the front of his house I pinned the metal 617 Squadron badge on his cardigan and left, with Lady Wallis driving me to the station. On 30 October 1979, just over a year later, he died. He was ninety-two that year and it was said he wanted to die. He had gone into hospital for rest, but nothing more, while there he passed away. He is today buried in St Lawrence churchyard, Effingham. A Vulcan of 617 Squadron flew over during the funeral on 3 November 1979.

Also in 1978, a memorable year for me, I spent three days at RAF Scampton with 617 Squadron, living in the very officers' mess the men of 617 had lived in during the raid on the dams. Little had changed with the hangars, typical of the Second World War. No. 2

Sir Barnes Wallis, 1978. © *Alan Cooper*

Last picture of Sir Barnes-Wallis. © *Alan Cooper*

The unveiling of the plaque outside the former home of Barnes Wallis in New Cross, South East London (author on the far left).
© *Hilda Cooper*

The grave of Sir Barnes Wallis

Hangar, the hub of 617 Squadron in May 1943, with Gibson's office overlooking 'Nigger's' grave where the dog had been buried and the briefing room, now the other ranks mess hall. The one difference was that Vulcans and not Lancasters were parked up on the runways. A Lancaster sat as gate guardian at the front gate, but it is now at East Kirkby. Because of the IRA threat, the turret guns front and rear were made of wood. I was lucky enough to be allowed inside and sit in the pilot's seat. The Lancaster was opposite the guardroom where 'Nigger' was taken after being knocked down outside the main gate.

Each day in the mess at about 1600 hours was tea time and on one of the days I was there the orderly, or duty officer came in and to my astonishment he looked just like David Maltby, I was so taken aback that I did not even speak to this officer, but over the years it has never left my memory.)

At RAF Scampton there was a small squadron museum with memorabilia including one of Guy Gibson's caps.

In 1979, a plaque was presented to the RAF Museum at Hendon in memory of Guy Gibson. This came from the wartime Dutch Resistance Fighters and is now on display at the museum. Also in 1979, George Brookes, the President of the Birmingham Dahlia Society, named a dahlia after Guy Gibson – it was salmon pink in colour. He also brought one out in yellow named after Barnes Wallis; both were eight to twelve inches tall. George himself had spent the war in another dangerous occupation, Bomb Disposal.

In 1980, a Memorial Service, attended by the Prince of Wales and over 1500 people, was held in memory of George at St Paul' Cathedral. (Author – I had the great honour of attending.) In January 1986, his wife Mary, known as Molly, joined him, they had lived in Effingham for forty-nine years. His house has now been renamed Little Court.

In April 1980, the reunion was held in Australia; where in Adelaide, 617 Squadron led the Anzac Parade, a plaque was laid at Adelaide airport and a commemorative tree. The inscription on the plaque read: 'Erected in memory of gallant comrades of the Royal Australian Air Force, who served in 617 Squadron, RAF 'Dam Busters' Squadron 1943–45. Lest we forget.'

In May 1980, a further reunion was held in Derby and organized by Derby County Council and Rolls Royce Limited, which of course powered the Lancaster bomber. Eleven survivors of the raid were present including Micky Martin. During the visit a poppy wreath was

Left to right; Webb, Townsend, Clay, Martin, Feneron, Buckley, Johnson, Foxlee, N/K, Howarth

dropped by a helicopter with Micky Martin on board – on the Derwent dam – in memory of the men lost on the raid. The veterans were paraded through Derby in vintage cars. A Vulcan of 617 Squadron made a flypast over the dam. In the same year a bust of Guy Gibson was presented by a Dutch couple to 617 Squadron Association.

In January 1981, a gold cigarette case which had been presented to Gibson in 1943 and inscribed ED 932-G, G.P.G, 17 May 1943,

A bust of Wing Commander Guy Gibson by Peter Close

Mick Martin and Bill Townsend at the Rolls Royce Derby, 1980

'Nigger' and 'Dinghy' was sold in auction at Sotheby's. The estimate on this was £600, but in fact went for £4,600.

A road on the South Canford Heath Estate, Poole, Dorset, was named after Guy Gibson and in Porthleven there is a road called Gibson Way.

On 26 September 1981, Freddie Tees was invited back to Bochum in Germany and the site of his crash in 1943. A memorial cross, which had been erected in Kohlinger Forest and instigated by the Hessen Scout Troop, was unveiled. Here, Freddie laid a wreath in respect of the dead. The cross was a sign of peace and freedom and the understanding between the two nations. After he died in March 1982, his ashes were taken to Germany and scattered where his crew are buried. (Author – I attended his funeral, a very moving occasion with playing of the *Dambuster March* during which I felt like leaving the room, but did not do so. I was so looking forward to him reading my first book on 617 Squadron but by two months he missed it.)

Matt Tees returns to the site of his crash

Also in 1981, Geoff Rice, a founder member of the 617 Squadron Association died.

(Author – In 1983, came the 40th Anniversary of the dams raid, with a week of celebrations in Lincoln. On this occasion it was a great pleasure and honour to meet Les Munro, who was over from New Zealand.)

On 29 September 1984, a blue plaque was unveiled at the former home of Barnes Wallis, No. 241 New Cross Road. Wallis had been awarded the CBE in 1943 and in 1968 made a Knights Bachelor. The plaque was put up by the London Borough of Lewisham. He had spent all his boyhood at this house and went to school at Haberdashers' Aske's School in New Cross at the age of six. It was from there that he, at the age of thirteen went to Christ's Hospital School. He left there at seventeen and returned to New Cross with no qualifications, so he started as a marine apprentice engineer at John Penn Street in Blackheath. It was in 1931 that he was commissioned to build an airship by Vickers and offered the job of chief assistant in the drawing office at Victoria. It was his R100 airship that was the most successful airship built in Britain. He retired in 1971 at the age of eighty-four.

In May 1987, at Woodhall Spa, the wartime home of 617 Squadron after leaving Scampton, a memorial was unveiled in the form of the Mohne Dam, on which there are the names of 201, 617 Squadron personnel who were killed in the war, including of course the fifty-three killed on the dams raid. During the occasion a photograph was taken of the choir from St Hugh's school, as they sat in front of the memorial a black Labrador dog turned up and sat in the middle of them, once the photograph had been taken the dog went away and was not seen again.

(Author – I am happy to say I helped with the names for this memorial. I was asked by a member of the 617 Squadron Association Committee to supply the names, post nominals for the men of 617 Squadron lost in the Second World War, but at the time I was dis-appointed that, for my efforts, I was not invited to the unveiling of the memorial. But today I am glad that my efforts bore fruit in making sure names and post nominals were not omitted, or misspelt.)

In 1988, Aleck, Guy Gibson's brother, who had served in the army during the war, died. His son Michael carried on the name Penrose Gibson, and Penrose was of course Guy's second Christian name.

In 1980, Gibson's medals were bequeathed to the RAF Museum by Eve Gibson and today lie alongside Mick Martin's medals. He died on 3 November 1988, age 70, the same day as Eve Gibson. Mick Martin stayed in the RAF and retired as Air Marshal Sir Harold Martin, KCB, DSO, DFC, AFC. In 1947, he broke the speed record for flying from England to Cape Town in a de Havilland Mosquito, for which he was awarded the Oswald Watt Gold Medal. He ended his RAF career in 1973 as Air Member of Personnel. He is today buried in Gunnersbury Cemetery. He had been knocked down by a bus outside Harrods's and was for some weeks in a coma, from which he never really recovered.

On 7 May 1990, a memorial was unveiled in the Steenbergen Park, it was the conception of Albert Postma and is a three-bladed propeller from a former 106 Squadron Lancaster, R 5697, which had crashed in Holland on 21 December 1942 and had been flown by Flight Sergeant George Anderson. On the memorial an inscription: 'For Our Tomorrow they gave Their Today, Lest We Forget.' Also on the memorial are the crests of 106 and 617 Squadrons. It was called the Gibson Warwick Propeller Memorial in Steenbergen.

This was unveiled by Group Captain Leonard Cheshire, VC, in attendance was Doug Jordan, Gibson's wireless operator when with

Gibson memorial, Steenbergen, Holland

Plaque to Gibson in Cornwall

106 Squadron and Mr G. van Wijk, the Burgomaster of Steenbergen.
The propeller was donated by 106 and 617 Squadrons. The idea of the
memorial was that of Albert Postma who had been a member of
the resistance and also fought at Nijmegen with the US 82nd Airborne
Division.

The medals of Guy Gibson VC, on display at the RAF museum, Hendon. © Alan
Cooper

In May 1990, the 47th Anniversary of the raid, members of 617 Squadron visited the Rolls Royce factory in Derby. They were driven through Derby in vintage cars, such as Bentleys and Rolls Royce, the whole of the centre of Derby was closed for this and the veterans, original Dambusters, men of the *Tirpitz* era, and post war, were given a tour of the Rolls Royce Factory. A special tie was designed for the visit and a painting of the attack on the dams. A Vulcan bomber – the Lancaster, for reasons of serviceability was not available – flew over Derby at a very low height and many people's windows were rattled on this occasion. The Vulcan of course was a post-war aircraft used by 617 Squadron.

After the visit Mick Martin wrote to Derbyshire Council who had organized the tour and said, 'You have made a lot of old men very happy.'

In 2009, the man who had played the part of Guy Gibson in the film, Richard Todd, died at the age of ninety.

Over the seventy years since the raid the number of survivors has dwindled.

Bill Townsend, CGM, died in 1991, aged 70. Ken Brown, CGM, died in Canada on 23 December 2002, aged 82. He had stayed in the RCAF until 1968, retiring with the rank of Squadron Leader. 'Big' Joe McCarthy, DSO, DFC, who also stayed in the RCAF after the war and reached the rank of Wing Commander, died aged 79 in 1998. Joe, with his son, went back to the Sorpe after the war and said if he had seen the Sorpe Dam before attacking it, he would never have thought it could be done.

Others who have died since the raid are, Ray Grayston, who died on 15 April 2010, aged 91, he had been Les Knight's flight engineer. George Chalmers, died 6 August 2001, aged 81, he had flown with Bill Townsend as his wireless operator having joined the RAF as a boy entrant. He remained in the RAF until 1954 with the rank of Flight Lieutenant. He went on to work for the MOD and was heavily involved in inflight refuelling for the RAF. Douglas Webb joined the RAF on his eighteenth birthday in 1940. He had flown as front gunner with Bill Townsend. After the war he became a photographer and worked on many films and TV series such as *The Sweeney*. Tony Burcher died in Tasmania in 1995. Pieces of his aircraft can now be seen at the RAF Museum Duxford.

On the death of Ray Grayston this left only four survivors of the raid in May 1943.

Bill Townsend and George Powell. © *Alan Cooper*

Each year, at the graveside of David Maltby, a service is held on the anniversary of his death in September 1943, this is organized by the East Kent Aircrew Association.

In Sherborne Church, Nottingham, is a plaque to 'The Glorious Memory of Henry Eric Maudslay, DFC, Squadron Leader, RAFVR. Killed in the attack on the Mohne Dam 16th–17th May 1943, aged 21 years'. This is on the wall to the left of the organ.

In the fishing village of Porthleven, Cornwall, there is a road called 'Gibson Way' and nearby in the main cemetery, the memorial to Guy Gibson. On it is 'Dedicated to Wing Commander Guy Gibson, VC, DSO, DFC, RAF 617 Squadron "Dambuster" on the 45th Anniversary of his death. Tues 19th September 1989'.

In the Mayor's Parlour at the Guildhall hangs a portrait of Guy Gibson, a Squadron plaque and a photograph of the breached Mohne Dam. He is also on the Porthleven War Memorial overlooking the harbour. A film was made of his time in Porthleven and shown there on 29 September 2004.

On 26 December 1990, another member of 617 Squadron who took part in the raid, Lance Howard died; he had flown with Bill

Members of the East Kent Aircrew Association at David Maltby's grave. © *Charles Foster*

Townsend on the raid and had flown twenty-five operations as a navigator when he joined 617 Squadron. He came from Western Australia in 1972 and was offered the MBE in the Birthday Honours, but he refused on the grounds that the award was to him and not on behalf of the RAAF Association for Western Australia and in recognition to the work done by the association. He died from heart problems that had developed during the war.

Tony Burcher died in Tasmania, where he went to live after living in Cambridgeshire for many years with his wife who was an ex-WAAF. After the war he received a 75 per cent pension from the Australian Government for a wartime back injury, but later this was upgraded to 100 per cent. He found the weather in the UK did not help his back problems.

Jim Fraser, who flew with Tony on the dams raid, died while flying a float plane near Saltey Bay, British Columbia, Canada.

In April 1993, David Shannon, who had played a major part in the dams raid died. Today there is a stone to commemorate his life in the churchyard of St Michael and All Angels, in Clifton Hampden, Oxfordshire, alongside a stone for his wife, Ann Somerset Shannon, who was a WAAF officer at RAF Scampton and died in 1990. Ironically, she died a day after her seventy-first birthday and he a month before his seventy-first birthday. On his stone is David John Shannon, DSO, DFC, RAAF, RAF 106 & 617 Squadron, below the squadron badge for 617 Squadron is the inscription The Dambuster.

In 1995, the RAF Scampton Museum Gallery was opened by Group Captain Burwell. It has many artefacts and pictures concerning RAF Scampton, not only the dams period, which of course is greatly covered, but all of its history.

In New Zealand, Les Munro became the Mayor of Te Tuti for several years. Today he is the only surviving pilot of the nineteen who set out in 1943. He attended the 60th Anniversary in May 2003 at RAF Lossiemouth, also attended by the Queen and Duke of Edinburgh. He also attended the 65th Anniversary held at the Derwent Reservoir. Two members of his crew, Bill Howarth, died in 1990 and Francis Rumbles in 1982.

Today there are only four men left alive of the 133 men who set out.

In May 2003, it was the 60th Anniversary of the raid. At the Eyebrook reservoir, Mr and Mrs Mobbs of Kettering, former members of the RAF and members of the Leicestershire and Rutland Ornithological Society, noticed commemorative plaques on the dam and decided that sixty years on, it should not go without being marked. She rang RAF Scampton and the idea was born to have a fly-past over the dam by the Battle of Britain Memorial flight, a wartime Lancaster bomber, and wartime Spitfire and Hurricane.

On 17 May 2003, the flight did a tour around Britain that included the Eyebrook, and Reculver in Kent, where Sir Barnes Wallis's son Christopher was present with many thousands of spectators.

Jim Heveron, who after the war became a Leader Training Commissioner and District Secretary to the South Wales Boy Scouts, was awarded the Silver Acorn, one of the Scouts' highest awards. Sadly, in 1994, he was taken into hospital for heart surgery but did not survive the operation. At his funeral the *Dambuster March* was played and the service conducted by an RAF Padre from RAF St Athan, who in the Second World War had been a Spitfire pilot. As he was giving the blessing two aircraft flew overhead, this had not been planned.

In 1996, plans were made to recover the remaining Upkeep bombs at Reculver. This was undertaken by Royal Engineers from the TA in Rochester, Kent. There were four, all of different sizes. While this was being done Sir Barnes Wallis's son Chris turned up. He was representing the Barnes Wallis Trust. One of the bombs was claimed by the Yorkshire Air Museum and is now on display there. In this case a full-size bomb.

In Adelaide, South Australia, a plaque was placed in memory of the South Australia Dam Busters. This memorial commemorates the bravery and heroism of three South Australian airmen who partici-pated in the famous Dam Buster raid on 17 May 1943:

Pilot Officer F.M. Spafford, DFC, Bomb Aimer, AJ-G Mohne
Flight Lieutenant R.C. Hay, DFC, Bomb Aimer, AJ-P Mohne
Flight Lieutenant D. Shannon, DFC, Pilot, AJ-L Eder Dam.

On 14 September 2010, a signed copy of Paul Brickhill's book *The Dambusters* was sold in an auction in Kent. It was signed by Flying Officer Brian Goodale, who had flown with David Shannon. It fetched £900.

Over the years many museums have been built and developed for the Dambusters they include the following:

RAF Scampton, now the home of the Red Arrows.
Derwent Valley.
Eden Camp, Yorkshire.
Brenzett Aeronautical on Romney Marsh, Kent, has a bouncing bomb.
Dambuster Inn, Scampton.
Reculver, Kent.
Duxford IWM, has a bouncing bomb.

In November 2012, in Gloucester, Squadron Leader Longbottom's medals, logbook and the key from the first live Upkeep bomb dropped before the dams raid, were sold at auction by the family. Sadly, he was killed in a flying accident in 1945, aged 29.

Wing Commander Guy Gibson's flying logbook now resides in the National Archives, previously the Public Record Office under the Air

4 series. Although still readily available to readers, it is kept in the safe for extra security; this is owing to documents being stolen in the past. This is a very valuable document, and irreplaceable. Some years ago a very good facsimile copy was produced by *After the Battle Magazine*, but is now out of print.

All aircrew had a flying logbook in which every flight – training or operations – was recorded after each flight. It recorded the hours flown and in the case of operations the target and any comments as to how the operation went. If it was the pilot, then he would put the names of the rest of the crew, if another member of the crew, then they would put the pilot's name. Each month the flight commander would inspect the log and sign it as a true statement of flights flown. When thirty operations had been flown and a tour of operations completed, the man was taken off operations and went into training, many aircrew found this more dangerous than operations. Some aircrew, rather than go into training, volunteered for the Pathfinders.

Sadly, in the case of some 55,000 aircrew in Bomber Command, an entry in red was put in the logbook with the following; 'missing', 'failed to return', or 'nothing heard since take off'.

Since the war many things have revolved around the dams raid. Such as a Carling Black Label TV Ad, with 617 Squadron flying over the dams and a German guard acting as a goalkeeper leaping up and down to catch the bouncing bomb, with the slogan 'Bet he drinks Carling Black Label' coming over on a simulated radio transmitter.

Sir Barnes Wallis and his wife were regular visitors to the Scafell Hotel, Borrowdale after the war. They always had the same room, No. 13. When the hotel was refurbished, rooms 13 and 11 were made into one and renamed the Barnes Wallis Suite in his honour. It was officially opened by his daughter, Mary Stopes-Roe.

In May 2011, Channel 4 made a documentary in which they tried to recreate the bouncing bomb; this was despite the vital workings from Barnes Wallis's papers being lost in flooding in the 1960s.

In May 2012 four men on motorbikes rode as near as possible to the route taken to the dams and laid a wreath at the Mohne Dam, this was organized by 'Help For Heroes'.

Probably the magic of the Dambuster raid will carry on for many years to come, what is it about this 'Airborne Commando' raid that intrigues people today seventy years later? Perhaps in a world war, an operation with a comparative small number of people, in amongst the large battles that were going on at the time. The names and background of the fighting men were not lost in great numbers, as was possible with the bigger battles. A wonderful black and white film of course enhanced its fame and prolonged its popularity.

The Author's memories

In 1980 I first visited the dams, Mohne, Eder, Sorpe and Ennepe and flew over them in a light aircraft at the lowest permitted height of 250 feet. I also visited many of the villages in the area of the dams, also, as a special treat, I went inside the Mohne Dam. When we landed near the Eder Dam we went for a coffee in the Waldeck Castle, or Schloss, overlooking the Eder Dam and now a restaurant. As we sat there I said to the pilot of the aircraft I had flown over the dams in, he himself a former Luftwaffe pilot, 'How would you like to fly and attack that dam, at night and at 60 feet?'

He paused and then said, 'They were either mad or brilliant pilots.' I now think we know the answer to that question.

Whilst in Germany I also spent a day with Dr Albert Speer at his home in Heidelberg, sadly he died a year later in London. He told me that he had not realized how much damage water could do. He praised the work of Bomber Command and said his only criticism was they had not done more of the Hamburg raids etc. if they had the war would have been over much earlier.

On my return to the UK I brought a message from Speer to Sir Arthur Harris, the contents I never saw, but I am sure that today it is in the Harris family memorabilia. I did try to get Dr Speer to come to the UK and speak to Harris about the bombing campaign and the affect it had on the war. He declined, so I was very surprised – as was Sir Arthur – to read that Speer was in London in 1979 for a TV programme and on returning to his hotel had died.

In 1982, my book was published by William Kimber and I am pleased to say has stood the test of time. To have a foreword by Air Marshal Sir Harold (Mick) Martin was a bonus beyond belief.

Just as an example of what research entails: I wanted to have the service details of all 133 men who took part in the dams raid, the officers records were at the time in London and I had no problem getting them, but when it came to NCO's it was a rather different story. Their records were kept at what was RAF Innsworth, Gloucester, but now an army barracks. They refused to let me have them so I went to my MP, an Ex-RAF pilot, Ivor Stanbrook. After a long process of back

Eder dam, post-war. © *Alan Cooper*

The 'Dambuster' helicopter flying over Derwent Dam, 17/05/80

and fore correspondence they let me have them, today I am so glad I pursued them.

In 1989, the first battlefield tour of the dams was headed by Holt's Battlefield Tours. I was asked to help set this up and be one of the guides, along with me was Len Sumpter, who flew with Dave Shannon on the dams raid. It was an honour and a great experience to sit next to Len for three days.

Len Sumpter at the grave of Guy Gibson, 1989. © *Alan Cooper*

In 1993, I again went on the dams battlefield tour with Holt's and again as a tour guide along with Len Sumpter, whom I had accompanied on the previous tour. To sit and talk to Len on this the 50th Anniversary was a great honour. A wreath was placed on the waters edge below the Mohne Dam. On this tour were five coaches, one with a party of ex-WAAFs all in their blazers and tartan skirts, the traditional dress of the WAAF Association.

The whole day of 17 May 1993, was covered by German TV. One of those present was Karl Schutte, a former gunner on the dam at the time of the attack and awarded the Iron Cross the next day, a man that Mick Martin greatly admired for standing his ground during the attack and always wanted to meet, but never did.

On the trip was Marna Young, John Hopgood's sister and also his niece Jenny, both wanted to meet Karl, the man that very likely shot down John's aircraft, this they did on the Mohne Dam and although Karl could not speak a lot of English it was a non-acrimonious occasion.

Karl Schutte after his Iron Cross presentation, 17 May 1943. © Karl Schutte

Marna Young, Hopgood's sister, and niece Jenny. © *Alan Cooper*

Karl Schutte meets Dambuster Len Sumpter. © *Alan Cooper*

We also found the Eder Dam covered in scaffolding. It had been found that the dam needed to have its stability improved. So perhaps, although repaired very quickly, there was a deep lying problem that had to be addressed in 1993/94.

CHAPTER 13

Was it a Success?

There were, and still are, people who say the dams raid was not a success and not worth the loss of life, even over the year's former members of 617 Squadron have had their doubts and said so publicly.

There was serious damage in the Ruhr and because of water losses there was also a loss of eight percent of steel output in the second half of 1943.

Whatever the men of 617 Squadron thought before or after the raid – which was during the height of the Battle of the Ruhr – it was a very successfully carried out operation in the heart of Germany, despite Goering's promise that 'No bomber would invade the Reich', it did give Germany a very 'bloody nose'.

The attack on the Ruhr area with its factories making war material such as tanks, aircraft and ammunition, all desperately needed by the front line troops, did make a difference, due to the loss of water, which to make steel and electricity one has to have.

It is also true that the dams were repaired within four months, but at what cost?

Dr Speer said several thousand men were brought from the making of the Atlantic Wall to repair the dams. Much of this wall was not built because of this, and in June 1944, when the invasion of Normandy took place, how much bearing did this have on the success of the invasion and the loss of life? Perhaps we shall never know, but wars are not won on one operation or battle, they all contribute. The sustained attack on the Ruhr industry by Bomber Command from March to July 1943, was yet another means of making sure Germany's war making industry was disrupted. There are some who thought that perhaps the dams raid would end the war and there were those who perhaps felt the dams raid was not a success and should not have happened. Sadly, we cannot roll back the clock in history and see the outcome, had it not taken place. This could apply to many things in war. But from Wallis's perspective it was his idea and belief that this would not bring the war to an end but at least shorten it.

Germany held concrete defences in great store and we have to say that in many cases this was to their advantage, so any way in making sure these defences were not built had to contribute to the war effort and bring it to an end.

If you look at any night in the long war that Bomber Command fought from September 1939 to 1945, there were losses every night, some higher than others, so if those eight aircraft and fifty-three men had not been lost on the dams raid, it's very likely they would have been risking their lives on normal bombing operations. With an operation at such low height, avoiding hanging cables and even trees, plus the ground defences, which in the case of flak ships who were moving all the time – such as in the case of Les Munro and his crew – even with the best planning is sometimes unavoidable. The slightest error in navigation could also be a crew's downfall.

Sir Arthur Harris, in his many after dinner speeches said, 'War is immoral', which of course is true and it's often the military people who do not want to go to war, as they know once you are in it, there is no turning back. But in the case of the Second World War, as opposed to many other previous wars and campaigns, with a dictator such as Hitler who could not be trusted, it had to be won. As happened in Europe, it would have been the same in the UK if Germany had been allowed to invade and this would have then left America isolated and with Japan, Germany would have taken over the whole world.

One has to praise the men of 617 Squadron and be ever grateful for their dedication and courage. They should never be doubted and the names of those 133 men must be etched in history for ever.

Mick Martin said it gave the British people hope at a time when we were certainly not winning the war. Giving the Germans a clout on the nose would show not only the British people, but the people in Europe, that there was hope for the future, and as long as they heard a British aircraft going overhead, the war was still being fought and despite what 'Lord Haw Haw' said on the radio, Britain, and now the USA, were going to make sure Hitler and his gang of Nazis were not going to succeed. It also did not do anything for the German morale that the Luftwaffe had not prevented this attack taking place.

It is surprising to read that although Sir Arthur Harris was not in favour of the dams raid, he was pleased when the two dams were breached. However, from his personal papers it would appear that in December 1943, only six months after the raid he said, 'For years we have been told that the destruction of the Mohne and Eder Dams alone would be a vital blow to Germany', but went on to say, 'I have seen nothing in the present circumstances or in the Ministry of Economic Warfare reports to show that the effort was worthwhile.'

In a private letter of January 1945 from Harris to Sir Charles Portal, the Chief of the Air Staff, Harris went on to say that the destruction of the Mohne and Eder Dams was said to achieve wonders, but it achieved nothing compared with the effort and loss.

On the other side of the coin when I visited the area of the dams in 1980 I was told, by the people who lived there, that it was the 'blackest night' of their lives and to tell them it was not a success was not an option.

War is evil, but sometimes is the lesser of two evils, and if the latter, is not evil in the eyes of God.

CHAPTER 14

One Day with Bomber Command

On 16 May 1943, at RAF Scampton, Lincolnshire, the air was full of throbbing aircraft engines of 617 Squadron.

On such a station as Scampton there were over 2000 men and women whose sole task was to get nineteen bomber aircraft and 133 aircrew into the air. They became the pioneers of victory in Europe and the ending of the war there.

A bomber station was like a self-contained town with its great number of buildings and network of roads connecting it all up.

The aircrew were like guests at a hotel, coming and going all the time. Some had finished a tour of operations, usually thirty, or sadly for some making that one-way trip and becoming casualties of war, either making the supreme sacrifice or spending the rest of the war in a German prisoner of war camp.

For every aircraft there were ten ground crew, each having a special trade and task, riggers, instrument repairers, armourers (known as 'bashers') and so on, but all vital to the maintenance of the aircraft and the safety of its crew. Each aircraft was checked before going out and checked on its return. On a Lancaster bomber there were twenty-four spark plugs to each engine, making a total of ninety-six in all, this was just one instance of the task they faced time and time again, often in foul weather, particularly bad in winter when ones hands are wet and cold, just a knock with a spanner would give great pain. All aspects of the aircraft were checked, engines, radios, hydraulics, no stone was left unturned.

The belts of ammunition were often done by WAAFs, sometimes assisted by air gunners – many a romance has started in this way –

10,000 rounds for the rear gunner and 2,000 for the mid-upper gunner.

The motto of the ground crew on a bomber station was, 'Keep them flying at all costs' and how well they kept to that motto.

While the air crew were trying to sleep and unwind, the station was filled with the sound of throbbing engines.

A briefing would be called for all crews operating that night, but until the curtain was pulled back in the briefing room they would not know the target, security was, and had to be, of the highest.

There were seven in a crew of a four-engine bomber, a pilot, navigator, wireless operator, flight engineer, bomb aimer and two air gunners. The pilot was the captain, but known as 'Skipper' or 'Skip' and flew the aircraft. The navigator had the important task of not only getting them to the target and back, but also on time, and not early, as hanging around in the target area, or trying to lose time on route was not to be encouraged. The flight engineer sat on a fold-up bucket seat opposite the pilot, his role was to make sure every drop of petrol was used in the most economical way. He also assisted the pilot on take-off, putting his hands under the pilot's on the throttles at the crucial time, as loss of power with a fully loaded up Lancaster would spell disaster. In general he made sure the aircraft flew safely – many a car mechanic, often having started as ground crew, were recruited for this role in the crew. The wireless operator had the task of keeping in touch with base, and in the event of having to abandon the aircraft, or ditch in the sea, his last message with their position could be crucial.

Each squadron had a commanding officer, a Wing Commander, in this case Guy Gibson. All his time would be taken up preparing nineteen aircraft and 133 men for the night's operation, but somehow he found time to take his own aircraft up for a routine air test. Then it was back to the ops room to meet the weatherman, intelligence officer, and many others who would contribute to the operations.

There were three other members of the crew, the bomb aimer, whose task was over the target, here he would be in sole charge of the aircraft to make sure the bouncing bomb was dropped in the right area.

The two air gunners, the rear gunner sat with his back to the rest of the crew in his own turret, or pod in today's terminology, and his only contact with the crew was on the intercom. As one gunner said, 'It gave you a sense of detachment sitting out beyond the tail of the aircraft and seeing nothing unless you turned sideways.' On the dams raid there was no mid-upper gunner, only a front gunner.

On seeing the signal to take-off, the pilot opened up the throttles and down the runway they roared with the four Merlin engines at full power, the flight engineer had his gloved hand underneath to make sure they stayed open. As soon as they were airborne the navigator would say, 'Hello Skip the course is …'

The pilot would reply, 'Hello navy on course' and so they set off to the target deep into Europe, the Ruhr dams.

Over the sea the gunners would test their guns and then report to the skipper all was well.

After dropping their bomb they then set a course for home. Back at base the watchtowers would be waiting for the first aircraft to arrive back. The wireless operator would call the watchtower operator, a WAAF, who would reply and repeat again, this was to make sure they had heard her. Each station had its own call sign. The pilot was told where to land, runway etc., or to circle while aircraft which had been perhaps damaged, or had engine trouble, could land ahead of him.

After landing the crews were taken to be interviewed by the station Intelligence Officer, he asked them questions such as, 'What was the Flak like?' 'Did you see any fighters or aircraft go down?' This was all to make sure the next operation in that area was hopefully made easier, all this would be recorded and brought out when the target was chosen. Finally to breakfast for the traditional aircrew bacon and eggs, and then, not to sleep but to a party.

Wing Commander Gibson had returned safely, but before he could go to bed or party he had letters to write – on this occasion no less than fifty-six – to the next of kin of crews who had not returned. Eight aircraft had failed to return.

All over the UK, telegram boys on red bikes would deliver a little yellow telegram that he carried in a leather case on his belt, it would say, 'I am sorry to inform you that your son, or husband, Sgt … is missing as a result of operations on … Letter follows'. This was the letter sent by Wing Commander Gibson. Sometimes, and some while later, there might be a further letter or telegram to say he was safe, but a prisoner of war, or to say that he had been killed. In this instance fifty-three were killed and three were prisoners of war.

This was a day like many days in the life of Bomber Command. Many more telegrams were sent, with 55,000 men being killed in

Bomber Command before peace would be won, but you can be sure that the men and women of Bomber Command more than played their part in the winning of peace in Europe.

This was the role of a bomber crew in the Second World War.

In the 1990s RAF Scampton was closed for a period of time, but re-opened and became the home of the Royal Air Force Aerobatic Team (The Red Arrows). The Control and Reporting Centre (CRC), No. 1 Air Control Centre (IAAC) and the Mobile Meteorological Unit.

For many years it had a gate guardian of a Lancaster, which is now at the former RAF East Kirkby.

Aircraft Used On The Dams Operation

ED 932-G   Flown by Guy Gibson.
Delivered to 617 Squadron on 30 April 1943, to 467 Squadron on 7 Feb 1945. To 61 Squadron on 27 Aug 1946. Scrapped on 29 July 1947.

ED 864-B*   Flown by Bill Astell.
Delivered to 617 Squadron on 22 April 1943. Only 22 hours on the clock.

ED 865-S*   Flown by Lewis Burpee.
Delivered to 617 Squadron on 22 April 1943. Only 17 hours on the clock.

ED 886-O   Flown by Bill Townsend.
Delivered to 617 Squadron on 23 April 1943. Lost on 11 December 1943. 138 hours on the clock.

ED 887-A*   Flown by Henry Young.
Delivered to 617 Squadron on 22 April 1943.

ED 906-J   Flown by David Maltby.
Delivered to 617 Squadron on 23 April 1943. Scrapped on 29 July 1947.

ED 909-P   Flown by Mick Martin.
Delivered to 617 Squadron on 23 April 1943. Scrapped on 29 July 1947.

ED910-C*   Flown by Warner Ottley.
Delivered to 617 Squadron on 28 April 1943. 20 hours on the clock.

ED912-N   Flown by Les Knight.
Delivered to 617 Squadron on 3 May 1943. Scrapped on 26 September 1946.

ED918-F   Flown by Ken Brown.
           Delivered to 617 Squadron on 30 April 1943. Crashed
           and burnt out 21 January 1944.
ED 923-T   Flown by Joe McCarthy.
           Delivered to 617 Squadron on 2 May 1943. Lost on 8
           September 1943. 75 hours on the clock.
ED 921-W   Flown by Les Munro.
           Delivered to 617 Squadron on 30 April 1943. Scrapped on
           26 May 1946.
ED 924-Y   Flown by Cyril Anderson.
           Delivered to 617 Squadron on 30 April 1943. Scrapped on
           23 September 1946.
ED 925-M* Flown by John Hopgood.
           Delivered to 617 Squadron on 30 April 1943. 17 hours on
           the clock.
ED 927-E* Flown by Robert Barlow.
           Delivered to 617 Squadron on 3 May 1943. 20 hours on
           the clock.
ED 929-L   Flown by Dave Shannon.
           Delivered to 617 Squadron on 30 April 1943. Scrapped on
           7 October 1946.
ED 934-K* Flown by Vernon Byers.
           Delivered to 617 Squadron on 3 May 1943. 13 hours on
           the clock.
ED 936-H   Flown by Geoff Rice.
           Delivered to 617 Squadron on 12 May 1943. Scrapped on
           28 July 1944.
ED 937-Z* Flown by Henry Maudslay.
           Delivered to 617 Squadron on 14 May 1943. 7 hours on
           the clock.

* Lost on raid

Awards for the Dams Operation Gazetted 28 May 1943 Presented by the Queen Mother on 22 June 1943

Victoria Cross
Wing Commander G.P. Gibson

Distinguished Service Order
Squadron Leader D.J.H. Maltby
Flight Lieutenant L.G. Knight
Flight Lieutenant J.C. McCarthy, DFC
Flight Lieutenant H.B. Martin, DFC
Flying Officer D.J. Shannon, DFC

Conspicuous Gallantry Medal
Flight Sergeant K.W. Brown
Flight Sergeant W.C. Townsend, DFM

Bar to the Distinguished Flying Cross
Flying Officer B. Goodale, DFC
Flight Lieutenant R.C. Hay, DFC
Flight Lieutenant R.E.G. Hutchinson, DFC
Flying Officer D.R. Walker, DFC

Distinguished Flying Cross
Flight Lieutenant J. Buckley
Flight Lieutenant L. Chambers

Pilot Officer G.S. Deering
Pilot Officer J. Fort
Flight Lieutenant H.S. Hobday
Flight Lieutenant C.L. Howard
Flight Lieutenant E.C. Johnson
Flight Lieutenant R.A.D. Trevor-Roper, DFM
Pilot Officer F.M. Spafford, DFM
Pilot Officer T.H. Taerum

Bar to Distinguished Flying Medal
Flight Sergeant C.E. Franklin, DFM

Distinguished Flying Medal
Flight Sergeant G.S. Chalmers
Flight Sergeant D.P. Heal
Sergeant G.L. Johnson
Flight Sergeant D.A. McLean
Flight Sergeant V. Nicolson
Flight Sergeant J. Pulford*
Flight Sergeant T.D. Simpson
Flight Sergeant L.J. Sumpter
Flight Sergeant R. Wilkinson
Sergeant S. Oancia
Sergeant D.E. Webb

* Not present at the presentation owing to sickness.

Index

211